WILLIAM HATFIELD

The Art of Creative Writing
An Inspirational Journey

Copyright © 2024 by William Hatfield

All rights reserved. No part of this publication may be reproduced, stored or transmitted in any form or by any means, electronic, mechanical, photocopying, recording, scanning, or otherwise without written permission from the publisher. It is illegal to copy this book, post it to a website, or distribute it by any other means without permission.

This novel is entirely a work of fiction. The names, characters and incidents portrayed in it are the work of the author's imagination. Any resemblance to actual persons, living or dead, events or localities is entirely coincidental.

William Hatfield asserts the moral right to be identified as the author of this work.

First edition

*This book was professionally typeset on Reedsy.
Find out more at reedsy.com*

To my wife, who has always been my biggest supporter and who has never doubted me, even when I doubted myself.

Contents

Foreword	iii
I Part 1: Foundations of Storytelling	
Chapter 1: Let's Begin	3
Welcome to the Craft - Where Whispers Become Worlds	3
Chapter 2: Narrative	16
Building Blocks of Narrative -	16
Where Myths Are Morphed into Masterpieces	16
Chapter 3: Voice	28
The Power of Voice - Where Echoes Become Anthems	28
Chapter 4: Characters	34
Crafting Captivating Characters - Where Ink Becomes Flesh and Blood	34
Chapter 5: Setting	53
Worlds Come Alive - Where Brushstrokes Breathe and Shadows Whisper	53
II Part 2: Mastering the Tools of the Trade	
Chapter 6: Plot	73
Plotting Your Path - From brainstorming to outlining:	73
Chapter 7: Dialogue	79
Dialogue's Dance - Where Words Become Music and Meaning Sings	79
Chapter 8: Nuance of Time	85

Time's Tapestry - Where Past and Present Weave a
Present Dance   85
Chapter 9:Description   92
    Where Paintbrushes Dance and Senses Sing   92
Chapter 10:Points of View   95
    Exploring different narrative perspectives   95
    Final words   102
    Unleashing Your Story - It's All Yours Now   102

About the Author   104

Foreword

So you want to be a creative writer.

Forget bland textbooks and dusty rules, aspiring bard! Dive headfirst into this portal where senses explode and imagination feasts. Within these pages, you'll crack open the treasure chest of storytelling, where captivating words pirouette like fireflies and worlds bleed from the ink, vibrant and alive.

No dry lectures here, no tedious formulas. We'll dance with metaphors, wrestle with plot twists, and paint portraits with prose sharper than any brush. You'll learn to breathe life into characters that leap off the page, their laughter echoing in your ears, their secrets whispering in the shadows.

This is an invitation to become an alchemist, transforming whispers into worlds, anxieties into adventures, and everyday moments into shimmering tapestries of fiction. We'll climb mountains of grammar, plumb the depths of emotion, and craft sentences that sing, sting, and soar.

Remember that time you devoured a book, devoured its world, its characters, its very soul? Let's create stories that do the same. Stories that linger in the reader's heart, warm embers in the hearth of their memory. Stories that become their escape, their solace, their secret whispered wish upon a star.

So, dear storyteller, are you ready? Ready to unleash the tempest within, to wield words like a sorcerer's staff, and weave narratives that dance in the moonlight? Then turn the page, and let the adventure begin. Within these pages lies not just a guide, but a portal. One that leads to a world where your imagination is the only limit, and your stories, the whispers that become legends.

The information about to be given within the following pages is a work of creativity that goes over many elements of storytelling that can be used in many forms. From novel writing to short stories, or even captivating introductions for anything that needs a little story to liven up everyday writing.

Part 1: Foundations of Storytelling

Chapter 1: Let's Begin

Welcome to the Craft - Where Whispers Become Worlds

Have you ever stumbled upon a dusty attic trunk, its hinges groaning open to reveal a treasure trove of forgotten dreams? Imagine, nestled amongst moth-eaten scarves and chipped teacups, you find a faded map scrawled with fantastical landscapes: shimmering mountains, whispering forests, and seas dotted with islands spun from spun sugar. This, my dear reader, is the invitation you hold in your hands, a map to your own attic trunk of imagination. Welcome to the craft of creative writing, where whispers morph into worlds and scribbles ignite into stars.

Over the next few chapters venture into the art of creative writing. Forget dusty classrooms and rigid grammar drills. Here, we wield words like paintbrushes, dipping them into vibrant palettes of emotion and experience. Learn the intricacies and nuance as we build the story, brick by brick, through so many of the important facets of creative writing. Forget the confines of "should" and "must." Here, the only rule is to follow the siren song of your own curious heart.

Think of a blank page as an artist's canvas, where ordinary ink transmutes into dragons and damsels, spaceships and soulmates. Each sentence, a whispered spell, conjures unseen landscapes and unheard melodies. With a twist of your pen, you become a weaver of dreams, a sculptor of realities yet to be imagined.

But don't mistake this journey for a solitary stroll. Here, you join a vibrant circus of storytellers, each voice a kaleidoscope of colors, each tale a shimmering thread woven into the grand tapestry of human experience. We gather around crackling campfires, swapping secrets and sharing fears, our laughter echoing through moonlit meadows. For in this haven of imagination, we are not lone adventurers, but a band of intrepid explorers, mapping the uncharted territories of our own creativity.

So, close your eyes and take a deep breath. Feel the ink dripping from your fingertips, the promise of possibility humming in the air. This is your invitation, adventurer. Step into the whispering world of words, where every comma holds a universe, and every full stop sparks a new beginning. Welcome to the craft of creative writing, where you are not just a reader, but a world-builder, a dream weaver, a storyteller, born anew.

The map is yours to unfold. The only question is, where will your imagination take you first?

The ink, still waiting to be poured from your imagination, a shiver of anticipation trickles down your spine. But where to begin? The blank page mocks you, a white sheet stretched across an endless horizon. Don't be daunted, my fellow explorer. Dive into the toolbox of possibilities!

Spark the Flame:

In the boundless realm of creative writing, we embark on a captivating odyssey—a voyage that unravels the intricate threads of memory, the vivid sensations of the senses, and the enigmatic art of eavesdropping. Welcome to a world where words paint pictures, emotions transcend the mundane, and stories whisper secrets waiting to be told.

Our first stop takes us deep into the recesses of memory. Like archaeologists of the past, we will unearth treasures buried within our own experiences. The Memory Match section is a portal to nostalgia, where childhood adventures

Chapter 1: Let's Begin

shimmer with forbidden magic, family secrets emerge as ancient scrolls, and grandparent's tales echo like haunting melodies. Here, we delve into the art of weaving personal narratives, infusing authenticity and emotion into our storytelling.

Next, we embark on a sensory safari—a vivid expedition guided by the senses. In this section, we close our eyes and let the wind's gentle whispers serenade our ears, feel the exhilarating rumble of distant thunder reverberate through our bones, and sit amidst the bustling cafe, where teacups clatter, and conversations form a cacophony of sensations. We become painters with words, translating sensory experiences into evocative descriptions that transport readers to the heart of our narratives. Prepare to taste, touch, smell, hear, and see the world as never before.

Our final destination is an intriguing one—we eavesdrop on the world, tuning into the symphony of humanity that surrounds us. Like silent detectives, we listen to the snippets of conversations on a crowded bus, observe the fleeting expressions on strangers' faces, and embrace everyday dramas as rich veins of inspiration. Here, we transform the world into our muse, letting its complexity and diversity breathe life into our narratives.

Uncover the magic of Memory Match, the allure of Sensory Safari, and the intrigue of Eavesdrop on the World. As we journey through these sections, your creative writing will transcend boundaries, and your stories will resonate with depth and authenticity. Let the adventure begin.

Memories:

Unearth the hidden gems within your own memories, embarking on a treasure hunt through the sands of time. For instance, picture those childhood escapades that glimmered with enchantment, where innocence intertwined with the uncharted. Remember the hushed family confidences, akin to ancient scrolls concealed in the attic's shadows. Recall the tales of your grandparents, echoing through generations like a haunting, timeless melody.

Now, let's delve into some specific examples of how to transform these memories into compelling narratives:

- **Childhood Adventures**: Suppose you have a vivid memory of exploring a mysterious, overgrown forest as a child. You can incorporate this by crafting a story where your protagonist embarks on a magical journey through an enchanted forest, drawing inspiration from the sense of wonder and curiosity you felt during your own adventure.
- **Whispered Family Secrets:** Imagine your family's hidden secrets revolve around an old, locked chest in the attic. You can use this as a central plot point in a mystery novel, where a character stumbles upon a similar chest, sparking intrigue and uncovering long-buried family mysteries.
- **Grandparent's Tales:** Your grandparents' stories about their youth can become the basis for a touching family saga. Create characters inspired by your grandparents and weave their tales of love, resilience, and adventure into a multi-generational narrative.
- **Romantic Rendezvous:** Long lost loves, or the one that got away. Use your past romantic memories as a tool for inspiration in your writing. In the hands of a skilled writer, it's a detonator, igniting desire and propelling the story forward with a force that rivals a supernova.

Imagine two souls, drawn together by an invisible thread, their paths crossing in a clandestine haven – a sun-drenched meadow bathed in golden dust, a crumbling library where shadows whisper secrets, a moonlit rooftop overlooking a city ablaze with dreams. These are the canvases upon which the rendezvous paints its masterpiece.

For it is not just the physical setting that ignites the spark. The rendezvous is a crucible where emotions crackle and ignite, where vulnerabilities are laid bare, and desires, once unspoken, find their voice. It's a dance of stolen glances and whispered confessions, of trembling fingers brushing and hearts pounding in unison.

But the rendezvous is not merely a sugary escape. It's a crucible of growth, a testing ground for love and courage. Can these stolen moments withstand the scrutiny of daylight? Will the truths whispered in the shadows hold their power when the sunrises? The rendezvous becomes a catalyst, forcing characters to confront their fears, their dreams, and the choices that lie ahead.

And the writer? He becomes the alchemist, weaving these elements into a tapestry of yearning, of anticipation, of the exquisite ache of desire. He paints the blush on a cheek, the tremor in a voice, the unspoken promises that dance in the air. He captures the breathless anticipation, the bittersweet joy, the echo of a touch that lingers long after the rendezvous ends.

So, the next time you pen a scene of stolen hearts and whispered secrets, remember the power of the "Romantic Rendezvous." It's not just a plot point, it's a portal, a doorway into the very core of your characters' souls. Let it be your brushstroke of passion, your whispered promise to your readers – a promise to ignite their hearts and leave them breathless, long after they've turned the final page.

By infusing your personal memories and experiences into your storytelling, you breathe life into your narratives, making them authentic, relatable, and emotionally resonant for your readers. These examples illustrate how the "Memory Match" technique can transform your past into compelling stories that captivate and engage your audience.

Sensory Safari:
Embark on a journey where your senses become your trusted guides, immersing your readers in a rich tapestry of sensations.

- **Sound:** Close your eyes and listen as the wind's gentle whispers through leaves serenade your ears, creating a soothing, natural melody. In your writing, capture the rustling leaves and the soft, calming hum of the wind, transporting your readers to a tranquil forest glade.
- **Touch:** Feel the exhilarating rumble of distant thunder reverberate through your bones, sending shivers down your spine. Translate this sensation into your narrative by describing the vibrations in the earth and the electrifying anticipation of a coming storm, allowing readers to feel the tension in the air.
- **Taste and Smell:** Sit in a bustling cafe, where the clatter of teacups and the symphony of conversations create a cacophony of sensations.

Describe the aromatic blend of coffee, the sweet scent of pastries, and the rich flavors that dance on the tongue. Engage your readers by evoking the taste and smell of this vibrant cafe scene.
- **Visual:** Become a painter with words, using your pen as your brush. Describe the colorful swirls of latte art, the warm, golden glow of the cafe's lighting, and the animated expressions of the patrons. Paint a vivid picture that transports your readers into the heart of the bustling cafe, allowing them to see the world you've created on the page.

By infusing your writing with these sensory experiences, you create a multi-dimensional narrative that enables your readers to taste, touch, smell, hear, and see the world you've crafted, making your storytelling more immersive and captivating.

Eavesdrop on the World:
Immerse yourself in the vibrant tapestry of humanity that envelops you. Assume the role of a silent observer, akin to a detective hunting for concealed treasures. As you navigate the city, pay heed to the snippets of conversations on a bustling bus; each sentence is a potential plot twist or a precious dialogue gem waiting to be unearthed.

- **Dialogue Gem:** On the bus, overhear a woman saying, "I never expected this adventure to lead me here." This snippet could inspire a character's unexpected journey in your narrative, adding intrigue.
- **Fleeting Expressions:** As you eavesdrop, notice the fleeting expressions on strangers' faces. Capture the wrinkled brows of a passenger lost in thought or the radiant smile of a child gazing out the window. These expressions can shape your characters' emotions and actions in your story.
- **Plot Twist:** In a cafe, you hear a man whisper, "I thought I'd lost it forever." This cryptic sentence can become a pivotal plot twist, revealing a character's hidden past or a long-lost item in your tale.
- **Everyday Dramas:** Embrace the everyday dramas around you, like the

barista comforting a tearful customer or the street musician serenading passersby. These real-life scenarios can infuse authenticity into your narratives.

By honing your eavesdropping skills, you transform the world into your muse, enriching your storytelling with the intricacies and diversity of the human experience. Let these hidden treasures breathe life into your narratives, making them relatable and engaging for your readers.

Craft Your Compass: Navigating the Writing Journey

Crafting a compelling story is akin to embarking on a grand adventure, and your compass for this journey is built on three essential components:

Genres

Your first task is to discover the genre that resonates with your heart's deepest desires. Imagine yourself standing at a crossroads where signs point to various literary landscapes. Do you hear the siren call of the thriller, beckoning with heart-pounding suspense? Perhaps you're drawn to the comedy lane, where laughter lights the path. Or maybe it's the emotional terrain of poignant human connections that stirs your soul. Identify your genre, and it will be your guiding star throughout your writing expedition.

Here are some examples:

- 1. Action & Adventure: Fast-paced thrillers filled with danger, escapes, and heroic deeds. Think pirates, treasure hunts, and daring missions.
- 2. Romance: Explores love stories in all their forms, from sweet first loves to steamy affairs to forbidden passions. Subgenres include historical, contemporary, paranormal, and more.
- 3. Mystery & Thriller: Keeps you on the edge of your seat with suspenseful plots, hidden clues, and unexpected twists. Popular subgenres include detective fiction, crime thrillers, and psychological suspense.
- 4. Science Fiction: Transports you to futuristic worlds, explores alien civilizations, and grapples with the impact of technology. Subgenres include dystopian fiction, space opera, and cyberpunk.

- 5. Fantasy: Immerses you in magical realms with mythical creatures, epic quests, and powerful spells. Popular subgenres include high fantasy, urban fantasy, and young adult fantasy.
- 6. Historical Fiction: Brings history to life through fictional stories set in specific eras. Subgenres include medieval, Victorian, American Civil War, and many more.
- 7. Horror: Thrills and chills with chilling stories of ghosts, monsters, and the supernatural. Subgenres include Gothic horror, cosmic horror, and psychological terror.
- 8. Contemporary Fiction: Explores everyday life, relationships, and challenges in the modern world. Subgenres include domestic fiction, coming-of-age stories, and social commentary.
- 9. Children's Fiction: Captures young imaginations with adventure, humor, and heartwarming stories. Subgenres include picture books, middle-grade fiction, and young adult novels.
- 10. Literary Fiction: Focuses on character development, beautiful prose, and exploration of complex themes. Often considered "highbrow" literature.
- Bonus Genres:
- Dystopian Fiction: Explores societies on the brink of collapse.
- Speculative Fiction: Encompasses genres that deal with hypothetical or fantastical situations.

Example: If you choose the mystery genre, imagine the thrill of unraveling an unsolved murder case in a sleepy, atmospheric town, each clue leading your characters closer to the shocking truth.

Characters

Your characters are the beating heart of your story. Dive deep into their essence. Explore the quirks and contradictions that make them uniquely human. What secrets do they guard? What vulnerabilities lie beneath their facade? The more intimately you know your characters, the more they come to life on the page, captivating your readers.

Chapter 1: Let's Begin

Example: Let's say you're crafting a character named Amelia, who appears confident and unflappable. Digging deeper, you uncover her fear of abandonment stemming from her childhood, adding layers of complexity to her persona.

Amelia, at first glance, was a symphony of steel and silk. Her emerald eyes, sharp as cut emeralds, held a gaze that could level mountains and make lesser souls squirm. Her smile, a rare and radiant thing, could charm vipers and soothe storms. Confidence clung to her like a second skin, tailored to perfection.

But beneath the polished veneer, a different story unfolded. Amelia's childhood, a tapestry woven with threads of neglect and whispered goodbyes, had etched a fear of abandonment onto her soul. It was a silent predator, lurking in the shadows of her every interaction, a cold hand forever gripping her heart.

This fear, this vulnerability, became the secret counterpoint to Amelia's outward bravado. It was the tremor in her hand when she reached for a handshake, the flicker of doubt in her eyes when praised, the ever-present need to prove herself, to earn her place in the sun.

Yet, this fear was not a weakness, but a crucible. It had forged her resilience, her unwavering determination. It was the fuel that propelled her to excel, to conquer, to become the unflappable woman she presented to the world.

In her pursuit of success, Amelia built fortresses of self-reliance. She surrounded herself with a curated circle of admirers, each carefully chosen for their perceived loyalty, their usefulness in her meticulously planned ascent. But within these self-constructed walls, she remained an island, her true self a solitary lighthouse casting beams of longing into the vast ocean of isolation.

Now, the story truly begins. A chance encounter, a whispered truth, a crack in the facade. Perhaps it's a confidante who sees through the polished exterior, a rival who exposes a hidden insecurity, or a love interest who dares to touch the untouchable.

This vulnerability, laid bare, becomes the catalyst for Amelia's transformation. It's a painful process, a shedding of the carefully constructed persona, a confrontation with the demons that have haunted her for so long. But it's also a chance at liberation, at forging genuine connections, at embracing the messy, beautiful complexity of being human.

So, Amelia's journey becomes one of peeling back the layers, of confronting the shadows and stepping into the light. It's a story of resilience and vulnerability, of conquering fear and embracing love. It's a testament to the human spirit's ability to rise from the ashes, stronger and more beautiful than ever before.

And in the end, Amelia, the woman who once wore confidence like a shield, discovers that true strength lies not in hiding the cracks, but in letting the light shine through them.

This is just the beginning of Amelia's story, a sketch in charcoal waiting to be brought to life with vibrant watercolors. It's a story that begs to be explored, a character who promises to keep you turning pages, eager to see what lies beneath the surface, what secrets the emerald eyes hold, and what kind of woman will emerge when she finally dares to be vulnerable.

Plot

The plot is the driving force behind your narrative. It's the mysterious whisper that beckons your characters forward. Plant a seed of conflict—a driving force that propels your characters into action. Create a ticking clock, a deadline that adds urgency to their mission. Introduce forbidden desires that entice and torment them. Your characters will dance around this plot element, drawn by its irresistible pull, and it will keep readers eagerly turning the pages.

Example: In a fantasy novel, the forbidden desire might be a powerful artifact that promises immense power but comes at a great personal cost, luring the protagonist into a moral dilemma.

Consider the following plot example:

Forbidden desire: Not an artifact, but a prophecy – a whispered promise that Christopher, a weaver by trade, will stitch together the threads of fate, uniting two rival kingdoms through a delicate marriage. But the tapestry of destiny is tangled, woven with the threads of two women:

Chapter 1: Let's Begin

Elara, the Sunborn: A fiery princess with hair like spun gold and eyes that hold the power of the sun. Her kingdom, bathed in perpetual twilight, yearns for warmth and light. Elara desires Christopher's hand, a union that could thaw the icy grip of winter.

Morwen, the Moonborn: A shadow dancer with eyes that shimmer like moonlight and a touch that chills the air. Her kingdom, shrouded in perpetual night, craves the sun's life-giving touch. Morwen sees Christopher as the key, a bridge between the two worlds.

Love's Dilemma: Christopher's heart, a tapestry of its own, struggles with the pull of both women. He sees Elara's fiery spirit reflected in his own passion for his craft, and he admires Morwen's quiet strength, akin to the intricate patterns he weaves. Yet, choosing one means betraying the other, jeopardizing the fragile peace between the kingdoms and risking the prophecy's unraveling.

Weaving Intrigue: As Christopher navigates the treacherous political landscape, his skills as a weaver become weapons. He spins lies and secrets, weaving alliances and sowing discord, all to keep the fragile peace from shattering. He navigates the gilded halls of both kingdoms, dodging courtly intrigue and dodging the jealous eyes of suitors vying for the hands of the princesses.

Personal Cost: The prophecy's whispers twist Christopher's dreams, haunting him with visions of a kingdom engulfed in flames or cloaked in eternal darkness. His love for both women becomes a burden, a constant reminder of the impossible choice he faces. The threads of fate bind him tighter, constricting his freedom and blurring the lines between love and duty.

Breaking the Pattern: As the day of the prophecy approaches, Christopher faces a desperate choice. Will he succumb to fate, weaving a tapestry of love that ignites the flames of war, or can he break free from the prophecy's grip, forging his own path and stitching together a future where love and peace prevail, even if it means defying destiny itself?

Threads of Fate promises a story of love and sacrifice, where the threads of destiny are not woven in the stars, but in the hands of a man who must choose between love and the fate of two kingdoms. It's a story that will leave you breathless, wondering if Christopher can untangle the threads of fate and weave a tapestry of his own making, where love becomes the ultimate power.

Setting

A novel isn't just words on a page. It's a world waiting to be explored, and the mapmaker, the architect, the conjurer of this world is the setting. It's the air you breathe, the ground beneath your feet, the symphony of sights and sounds that whispers the story's secrets.

Imagine a detective story trapped in a sterile white room. No flickering gaslight, no rain-slicked cobblestones, no whispers in smoky alleys. Where would the mystery cling? How could tension coil in the air when there's only sterile silence? The setting breathes life into the chase, paints shadows on the culprit's face, makes the rustle of a cloak a harbinger of danger.

Now, picture a sweeping romance blooming in a concrete jungle. Where would stolen glances find refuge? Where would whispered promises echo? The setting paints a backdrop of stolen moments under starlit skies, entwined limbs on windswept cliffs, laughter dancing in moonlit gardens. It becomes the confidante, the witness, the canvas on which their love story unfolds in vibrant hues.

Setting isn't just window dressing. It's the alchemist, transforming words into experiences. It can be the oppressive heat of a desert that whispers madness, the salty tang of the sea that carries whispers of longing, the hushed reverence of a library that cradles secrets in dusty tomes. It's the language the characters speak before ever uttering a word, the pulse of the story beneath the surface of plot and dialogue.

So, the next time you lose yourself in a novel, remember: you're not just reading words, you're breathing the setting's air, feeling its pulse, hearing its whispers. It's not just the story happening, it's the world itself telling you its tale, one detail, one sensation at a time. Because without the setting, the novel is just ink on paper. With it, it's a universe waiting to be lived.

Remember, dear adventurer, the path is rarely straight.

Embrace the unexpected twists and turns in your writing journey. Sometimes, a wrong turn can lead to the most exciting discoveries. Each misstep is a brushstroke on your canvas, shaping your story into something uniquely yours. As you grab your pen and ignite the spark of your imagination, let the whispers of genre, characters, and plot guide you through the literary landscape. The world awaits your story, one word at a time.

With this compass in hand, you're ready to embark on a writing adventure that will captivate and enchant your readers.

Chapter 2: Narrative

Building Blocks of Narrative -

Where Myths Are Morphed into Masterpieces

Ah, the narrative! The scaffolding upon which our fantastical worlds hang, the intricate dance of elements that breathes life into whispered dreams. But fear not, fledgling architect of fiction, for the building blocks of this majestic mansion are not cold stones and mortar, but the very essence of stories themselves.

Welcome to the grand construction site of storytelling, where we build worlds from whispers and dreams. As you embark on this creative journey, remember that the foundation of your narrative is not stone and mortar but the essence of stories themselves.

First, we lay the cornerstone - plot. Is it a whirlwind romance unfolding in a Parisian cafe, a detective's hunt for a phantom thief in a gaslit London, or a spaceship crew's desperate struggle against interstellar oblivion? Define the journey, the central conflict that will propel your characters forward, their hearts pounding with purpose.

Plot:

Chapter 2: Narrative

- Think of the plot as the cornerstone of your literary mansion. Consider it a roadmap that guides your characters through a captivating journey. Whether it's a passionate romance in a Parisian cafe, a thrilling hunt for a phantom thief in gaslit London, or a desperate struggle against interstellar oblivion, define the central conflict that propels your characters forward.
- *Example*: In a fantasy adventure, your plot could revolve around a young hero's quest to retrieve a stolen magical artifact before it falls into the hands of a power-hungry sorcerer.
- Next, we carve the figures who move across this stage - characters. Not mere puppets spouting dialogue, but living, breathing beings with flaws and fire in their hearts. Craft their backstories, the whispered secrets that haunt their shadows, the dreams that shimmer just out of reach. Let their choices, their mistakes and triumphs, be the brushstrokes that paint your narrative landscape.
- Characters:
- Characters are the lifeblood of your narrative. They're not just dialogue-spouting puppets but living, breathing beings. Craft their backstories, quirks, and aspirations. Unearth the secrets that haunt their shadows and the dreams that tantalize their hearts. Your characters' choices, mistakes, and triumphs are the strokes that paint your narrative canvas.
- *Example*: Develop a complex character like Jane, a brilliant scientist with a paralyzing fear of failure, torn between her ambition and the need to save her endangered family.
- Now, we paint the backdrop - setting. Is it a sprawling cyberpunk metropolis where neon signs bleed into the twilight, a sun-drenched village nestled amidst whispering rice paddies, or a moonbase carved from lunar ice? Immerse your reader in the sights, sounds, and smells of this world, let the humidity cling to their skin, the desert wind sting their eyes. Make them feel the ground beneath their characters' feet, real and tangible as the words on the page.
- **Setting:**
- The setting serves as the backdrop against which your story unfolds. Whether it's a neon-lit cyberpunk metropolis, a serene village amidst rice

paddies, or a lunar ice-carved moonbase, immerse readers in this world. Make them feel the environment—the humidity clinging to their skin, the sting of desert winds in their eyes. Your setting should be as real and tangible as the words on the page.
- *Example*: Transport readers to a mystical forest where ancient trees whisper secrets, and bioluminescent creatures light the path of your characters on a quest for ancient wisdom.
- But a beautiful shell needs a beating heart. That's where theme steps in, the soul that whispers beneath the surface. Is it about the enduring power of hope, the destructive grip of revenge, or the bittersweet dance of mortality? Let your theme resonate through every beat of your story, a subtle melody that lingers long after the final page is turned.

Theme:

- Theme is the soul of your narrative, the underlying message that lingers. It can be about hope's enduring power, the destructive nature of revenge, or the poignant dance of mortality. Infuse your theme into every narrative beat, creating a subtle melody that resonates long after the final page.
- *Example*: If your theme is the resilience of the human spirit, explore how your characters persevere through adversity, finding strength in their vulnerabilities.
- And finally, there's the lens through which your world is seen - point of view. Will you weave your tale through the eyes of a jaded detective, a wide-eyed child who sees magic in the mundane, or an omniscient narrator who whispers from the shadows? Choose your storyteller wisely, for they are the bridge between your world and the reader's imagination.
- **Point of View:**
- Choose the lens through which your readers experience your world. Will it be through the eyes of a jaded detective, a child who finds magic in the mundane, or an omniscient narrator with a penchant for shadows? Your storyteller bridges the gap between your world and the reader's imagination.

- *Example*: Selecting a first-person perspective from a child's point of view can provide a fresh and innocent outlook on a fantastical adventure, adding charm and wonder to the narrative.

Remember, these building blocks aren't rigid; they're living, breathing bricks ready for your touch. Experiment, mold them, and create a narrative that sings. Let your plot twist and turn, your characters surprise, your setting enchant, your theme resonate, and your point of view dazzle with kaleidoscopic perspectives. The world of storytelling awaits your architectural genius.

Remember, apprentice architect, these blocks are not rigid pillars, but living, breathing bricks waiting to be molded. Experiment, twist them, shape them to build a narrative that sings. Let your plot twist and turn, your characters defy expectations, your setting become a character in itself, your theme pulse with hidden meanings, and your point of view dance with kaleidoscopic perspectives.

For in this craft, the only rule is to break the rules. So go forth, storyteller, and build your narrative palace, brick by vibrant brick, word by whispered word. Remember, the finest masterpieces are born not from cold blueprints, but from the flames of your own imagination. The world awaits your architectural artistry. Let the building begin!

The foundations laid, our narrative mansion rises, floor by floor, filled with the echoes of laughter and whispers of intrigue. But wait, adventurer, for within these walls are hidden chambers, secret passageways waiting to be unlocked. Let's explore!

Level Up Your Plot:

Consider a novel where the main plot is a detective solving a crime. A subplot could involve the detective's strained relationship with their teenage son. This subplot not only adds emotional depth but also mirrors the main plot's theme of uncovering hidden truths. It's like a painter using both dark and light shades to create a more dynamic and engaging picture, where each color enhances the others.

Your story is like a tapestry, where each thread is a subplot. Like a river's tributaries, these subplots meander, enriching the landscape. For instance, in a mystery novel, a subplot could be the detective's personal life, providing a contrast to the main crime-solving plot and adding emotional depth. This is akin to a painter using varied hues to add texture to a canvas.

Subplots as Woven Threads:

Think of your main plot as the central river. Subplots are like the streams that feed into it, each bringing its own narrative and emotional depth. For instance, in a detective story, a subplot could explore the detective's personal struggles, perhaps a family dilemma, which parallels and enriches the main theme of searching for truth. It's like adding different colors to a painting, each subplot a different shade that enhances the overall picture and provides a more immersive experience for the reader.

The Ticking Clock for Suspense:

Imagine your story's tension as a ticking clock, each tick heightening the sense of urgency. This could manifest as a deadline for a character to achieve a goal, such as finding a cure for a disease in a medical drama, where each moment lost is a step closer to disaster. The ticking clock is like the beating of a drum, each beat increasing in speed, compelling the characters to act with urgency and the readers to turn the pages faster. Envision a ticking clock hanging over your story's world, its ticking resonating with impending urgency. This could be a literal deadline, like a character having 24 hours to solve a puzzle, infusing each moment with tension and driving the narrative forward. Think of it as a drummer setting a relentless rhythm, compelling dancers to move faster.

Twists and Turns for Engagement:

Envision your plot twists as the magician's flourish, surprising and delighting the audience. A well-placed twist can be like finding out the quiet character in the corner is actually the mastermind, or the villain is revealed to have noble intentions. These twists are the narrative equivalent of a magician's reveal - the moment the audience gasps in surprise, their perceptions entirely flipped. Effective plot twists are like hidden passages in a maze, leading the reader down a path they never expected but find utterly compelling. Like a magician's sleight of hand, these plot twists should surprise and delight your readers. A trusted friend revealed as the villain, or an enemy who turns out to be an ally, can flip the story on its head. It's the gasp of the crowd when the unexpected happens, keeping them on the edge of their seats.

Flesh Out Your Characters:

Beyond Biographies: Don't just tell us their age and hair color. Dig deeper. What hidden fears gnaw at them? What dreams shimmer just out of reach? Reveal these vulnerabilities, these contradictions, and your characters will leap off the page, their humanity resonating with every reader.

In creative writing, it's crucial to explore the layers of a character's psyche, much beyond the superficial traits. Let's take the character of Emily, a seemingly successful corporate lawyer. At first glance, she's defined by her sharp suits and flawless track record. But delve deeper, and you'll find a mosaic of fears and aspirations that make her vividly real.

Emily, despite her external confidence, harbors a deep-seated fear of failure, stemming from a childhood overshadowed by a highly successful parent. She lies awake at night, haunted by the thought that one wrong move could unravel her carefully constructed image. Her dream, shimmering just out of reach, is not another courtroom victory but the yearning to pursue her passion for painting – a desire she suppresses for fear of not living up to expectations.

In one scene, we could show Emily standing before a blank canvas in her rarely-used home studio. Her hand trembles as she holds the brush, a symbol of her unspoken dreams. The juxtaposition of her confident courtroom persona with this vulnerable moment at the canvas offers readers a glimpse into her complex inner world. It's these contradictions and vulnerabilities that breathe life into characters, making them resonate with readers who see reflections of their own fears and unfulfilled dreams.

By focusing on these inner conflicts and hidden desires, we create characters who are not just entities moving through a plot, but living beings with whom readers can empathize and connect on a deeper level.

Motivation's Melody:

Characters don't move on whims. Define their desires, their deepest needs, the driving force behind every action. Let their motivations hum beneath the surface, propelling them forward, even when their paths are shrouded in confusion.

In the tapestry of storytelling, character motivation is the invisible thread that weaves through every action, decision, and word. It's the heartbeat of your characters, driving them towards their destiny. Let's take an example to illustrate this concept:

Consider the character of Elena, a young, aspiring journalist in a dystopian society. Her driving motivation is the search for truth in a world shrouded in lies and propaganda. This deep-seated need stems from her childhood, where she witnessed the unjust disappearance of her activist parents.

Elena's every action, from sneaking into forbidden zones to interviewing rebels, is fueled by this unquenchable thirst for truth and justice. Her desire to expose the corrupt system is not just a goal; it's a necessity that defines her existence. Even in moments of doubt or danger, this inner motivation keeps her moving forward, her resolve unwavering.

As she uncovers layers of deception, her journey becomes more perilous. Yet, it's her motivation that acts as her compass, guiding her through the labyrinth of intrigue and peril. Elena's story becomes a melody of motivation, a symphony of purpose and determination that resonates with readers, inspiring them to consider the power of truth in their own lives.

By crafting a character with such profound motivation, you create a narrative that pulsates with life, drawing readers into a world where every step is a testament to the character's indomitable spirit.

Dialogue Delights: Let your characters dance with words! Craft dialogue that crackles with wit, drips with vulnerability, or simmers with unspoken tension. Make their voices unique, their rhythms echoing their personalities.

In the world of creative writing, dialogue is not just about exchanging information. It's a dance of words, a symphony of voices that reveals the depths of your characters. Let's take an example to illustrate this concept:

- **Crackling with Wit**: Imagine a character, Alex, known for their sharp wit. In a scene at a dinner party, Alex quips, "If intelligence were a crime, I'm afraid this party would be law-abiding." This line not only elicits a laugh but also subtly highlights Alex's disdain for the superficiality around them. Their dialogue is a mirror to their intellect and perspective, making their every word a reflection of their sharp mind.
- **Dripping with Vulnerability**: Now consider Emma, a character grappling with personal loss. In a quiet moment, she confesses to a friend, "Every night, I set the table for two, forgetting for a moment he's gone." This simple admission reveals her deep-seated pain and longing, her words painting a picture of her inner turmoil. Emma's dialogue doesn't just tell us about her loss; it lets us feel her heartache.
- **Simmering with Unspoken Tension**: Finally, take two characters, John and Sarah, with a complicated past. In a charged scene, John says, "It's cold in here." Sarah replies, "Maybe it's not the room." The dialogue here is layered. It's not about the temperature; it's a veiled reference to their strained relationship, the chill between them palpable.

In each example, the dialogue is more than words exchanged. It's a window into the souls of these characters, their fears, desires, and histories unfolding in every spoken word. This is the art of crafting dialogue that truly delights.

Flaws and Follies: Nobody's perfect. Embrace your characters' imperfections, their jealousies, their rash decisions. These flaws make them relatable, their struggles mirroring our own.

Character flaws are not just mere shortcomings; they are the intricate threads that weave the fabric of a compelling narrative. Embracing these imperfections is key to crafting characters that resonate with readers on a profound level.

Let's consider the character of Clara, a brilliant but impulsive detective. Her intelligence is her strength, but her impatience often leads to rash decisions. For example, in a pivotal scene, Clara disregards protocol to follow a hunch, leading to a critical confrontation with the antagonist. However, this act also inadvertently jeopardizes the safety of her team.

Clara's flaw – her impulsivity – adds layers to her character. It makes her human, fallible, and relatable. Her flaw drives the plot, creating tension and conflict. It also opens avenues for character development; as she faces the consequences of her actions, Clara learns the value of patience and teamwork.

Through Clara's journey, readers see a reflection of their own struggles with impulsivity or rash decisions. Her imperfections make her more than just a character in a story; they make her a mirror to the human condition, highlighting the complexity and duality of our nature.

Craft Your Canvas

Sensory Symphony: Don't just describe, evoke! Let your reader feel the rain stinging their cheeks, the sand crunching under their boots, the warmth of a lover's breath. Paint your setting with vibrant sensory details, making it a world they can taste, touch, and smell.

In the art of creative writing, sensory details are the brushstrokes that paint a vivid world for the reader. It's about creating an immersive experience that transcends mere description. Let's dive into a scene to illustrate this 'Sensory Symphony':

Imagine a protagonist, Elise, wandering through an ancient forest. As she treads softly, the earthy scent of damp moss fills the air, a subtle reminder of the forest's age and wisdom. The leaves rustle gently above, whispering secrets of the past. Each step Elise takes, the soft, spongy ground yields under her hiking boots, a tactile contrast to the city's hard concrete she's used to.

Suddenly, a light drizzle begins. The raindrops kiss her cheeks softly at first, then grow more insistent, like a passionate, unspoken plea from the sky. She can taste the freshness of the rain, each drop a tiny burst of life on her tongue. In the distance, a flash of lightning briefly illuminates the forest, casting eerie shadows that dance around her.

As night falls, the air cools. The aroma of pine becomes more pronounced, mingling with the petrichor. Elise wraps her jacket tighter around her, feeling the cozy warmth against her skin, a comforting embrace in the vast, wild forest.

In this scene, every sensory detail is meticulously chosen to not just describe Elise's surroundings, but to transport the reader there, to make them feel the forest's embrace, hear its whispers, and smell its ancient scents.

Show, Don't Tell: Let the setting become a character, whispering secrets and foreshadowing events. A creaking floorboard, a flickering candle, a lone crow silhouetted against the moon – these details speak volumes, adding depth and mystery to your world.

In the craft of storytelling, the setting is not just a backdrop; it's a living, breathing entity that can add layers of depth and intrigue to your narrative. Imagine a scene set in an old Victorian mansion, where every element of the setting tells a part of the story.

As our protagonist, Sarah, steps into the mansion, the floorboards groan under her feet, each creak a whisper from the past, hinting at the secrets hidden within these walls. The mansion, with its high ceilings and shadowy corners, feels like a character itself, watching Sarah with a hundred unseen eyes. The wind howls outside, rattling the windows, as if trying to communicate a warning.

In the dimly lit hallway, a candle flickers, casting dancing shadows on the walls. This flickering light not only sets a somber mood but also symbolizes the uncertainty that Sarah feels as she delves deeper into the mystery of the mansion.

Outside, a lone crow is silhouetted against the full moon, its solitary figure adding a sense of foreboding. The crow's caw echoes in the stillness, a sound that seems to carry a message from beyond.

In this scene, the setting itself becomes a storyteller, using sensory details to evoke emotions and foreshadow events. The creaking floorboards, the flickering candle, and the lone crow all work together to create an atmosphere of suspense and mystery, drawing the reader deeper into the world of the story.

Worldbuilding Wonders: Whether it's a fantastical kingdom or a dystopian megacity, flesh out your setting with intricate details, unspoken rules, and a history that whispers through the cracks. Make it real, make it breathe, and your reader will become a willing citizen of your world.

Remember, architects of imagination, these are not rigid formulas, but tools to play with, bend, and break. Experiment, surprise yourself, and let your narrative evolve organically. For in this ever-shifting mansion, the truest magic lies not in strict blueprints, but in the serendipitous discoveries you make along the way. So keep exploring, keep building, and watch your story unfold, room by wondrous room, into a masterpiece that sings with your unique voice. The world awaits its grand unveiling.

Worldbuilding is the art of creating a universe that breathes life into your narrative. Let's venture into a new world that was crafted:

The city of Veridian, a neon-lit megacity with a heartbeat of its own.

Veridian is not just a setting; it's a character in its own right. The city's towering skyscrapers, draped in neon signs, cast a perpetual twilight over the streets. Rain falls in a perpetual drizzle, creating a symphony on the metal rooftops, while the aroma of street food blends with the industrial tang in the air.

The city has its unspoken rules. In the bustling marketplace, vendors and thieves speak in a secret language of gestures, a tradition passed down through generations. The upper echelons of the city live in floating skyscrapers, disconnected from the grim reality below, where the poor scrape a living in the shadows of their opulence.

Whispers of Veridian's past echo in its architecture – the ancient ruins beneath the modern layers tell stories of a bygone era, of revolutions and fallen heroes. Holographic street art adorns old walls, blending history with the pulse of modern rebellion.

As you delve into the alleys of Veridian, you discover its true magic – the resilience of its people, their dreams and struggles, painting a picture of a world both fantastical and deeply human. The reader becomes a citizen of Veridian, navigating its complexities, feeling its pulse, and witnessing its tales unfold.

Chapter 2: Narrative

This world is not just a backdrop for action; it's an integral part of the story, evolving and growing with every chapter. It's a testament to the power of imagination, a world that lives and breathes beyond the confines of the page.

Chapter 3: Voice

The Power of Voice - Where Echoes Become Anthems

Voice is a tricky concept to weave throughout your story. But when the voice rings true, the magic happens. You forget you're reading, you become immersed in the lives unfolding before you. You laugh with the characters, cry with them, rage with them, their voices echoing in your own heart. That's the power of voice – to transport you, to challenge you, to make you believe that these fictional beings are breathing, living, right beside you.

Let the words that flow before you be the workshop where whispers morph into anthems! We've laid the foundation, built the walls, and breathed life into our characters and worlds. Now, it's time to climb to the rooftop, dear friend, and let the wind of your unique voice sing across the narrative landscape.

For voice, you see, is the soul of your story, the unseen brushstroke that colors every sentence, the melody that hums beneath the surface. It's the twinkle in your narrator's eye, the grit in your heroine's teeth, the whimsical twist in your world's description. It's the reason your reader turns the page, eagerly awaiting the next note in your song.

But finding your voice, like catching fireflies in a summer twilight, can be a slippery dance. Fear not, for these tips are your fireflies, shimmering beacons to guide you on your quest:

Narrative voice is the magic spell cast by writers, the invisible ink that binds words to emotions, and the conductor in the orchestra of a story. It shapes how we experience the narrative, whispering secrets in our ears or shouting proclamations from the rooftops. Let's explore two distinct voices, each a unique instrument in the storyteller's toolbox:

1. The Intimate Confidante:

This voice is a close friend, pouring their heart out in a hushed tone. We're drawn into their thoughts and feelings, privy to their vulnerabilities and triumphs. Imagine Holden Caulfield in "The Catcher in the Rye," his cynical humor masking a deep yearning for connection, or Scout Finch in "To Kill a Mockingbird," her innocent eyes capturing the complexities of racism in the American South.

Example:

"The rain lashed against the window like a thousand tiny ghosts, mimicking the rhythm of my racing heart. My hands trembled as I clutched the letter, the words blurring through unshed tears. How could he leave? After everything we'd been through, all the promises whispered in the moonlight, was it all a lie?"

This voice creates empathy, drawing us into the character's emotional landscape. We feel their pain, share their joy, and become invested in their journey. It's like curling up by a crackling fire, listening to a trusted friend confess their deepest desires.

2. The All-Knowing Witness:

This voice is a detached observer, a fly on the wall witnessing the grand tapestry of life unfold. It knows everything, past, present, and future, offering panoramic views and insightful commentary. Picture the omniscient narrator in Gabriel García Márquez's "One Hundred Years of Solitude," weaving generations of the Buendía family into the fabric of Colombian history, or the dry wit of Nick Carraway in F. Scott Fitzgerald's "The Great Gatsby," chronicling the opulent decay of the American Dream.

Example:

"The city sprawled beneath them, a glittering beast pulsating with life. Towers of steel scraped the clouds, their windows reflecting the dying embers of the sunset.

In a penthouse at the apex of this concrete jungle, Jay Gatsby, a man woven from ambition and secrets, hosted a symphony of extravagance. Little did he know, the night held more twists than the champagne corks popping in his lavish party."

This voice creates a sense of awe and wonder, inviting us to marvel at the grand forces at play. It offers perspective, highlighting the irony and humor in human struggles, and reminding us of the vastness of the world beyond our own experiences.

These are just two of the many voices a writer can wield. Each one, whether introspective or panoramic, shapes the reading experience and imbues the story with its own unique soul. So, the next time you dive into a book, listen closely to the voice that guides you. Is it a whispered secret or a booming chronicle? Let its melody carry you away, and witness the magic of narrative voice unfold.

Embrace the Echoes:

Your voice isn't born in a vacuum, it's a chorus of influences. Let the authors you adore whisper in your ear, their styles and rhythms becoming brushstrokes on your own canvas. But remember, dear artist, to add your own color, your own unique twist to the melody.

Don't fear the ghosts in your library, whisperer of words. Those towering shelves aren't tombstones, but echoing caverns where literary giants dance. Let Austen's wit brush you with its feather-light touch, Hemingway's punch land crisp on your prose. Hear Dickens' symphony of voices orchestrate your scene, feel Woolf's waves of consciousness ebb and flow within your narrative. These whispers, they're not shackles, but pigments on your palette, brushstrokes on your canvas.

But, oh, artist of language, never be a mere copyist! Dip your quill in your own inkwell, let your soul color the borrowed shades. Weave Tolkien's epic scope with a dash of Murakami's surreal quirk. Infuse Atwood's social scalpel with Pratchett's fantastical whimsy. Let your voice be a mosaic, each tile an echo, yes, but each bearing the unique stamp of your soul.

For your story, dear writer, is not a plagiarized echo, but a symphony spun from a thousand threads. It's the waltz of Austen's wit played on a banjo carved from Twain's wit, the roar of Hugo's revolutions whispered in Plath's confessional poetry. It's yours, a singular melody rising from the chorus, a brushstroke of your own fire on the canvas of time.

So embrace the echoes, creator of worlds. Let them guide your hand, but never silence your heart. Paint your story with the borrowed hues and your own vibrant soul, and in that tapestry, you'll find the only voice that truly matters – your own.

Listen to the World:

The symphony of human experience is your richest musical source. Tune into the rhythm of conversations on a bustling street, the bittersweet lilt of a forgotten melody, the raw emotions whispered in a lover's sigh. Let these sounds seep into your words, adding authenticity and depth to your voice.

Don't just read the world, listen to it. Press your ear to the concrete symphony of the city, let the frantic tap-dance of heels and the guttural rumble of engines paint percussion marks on your soul. Lean in to the bittersweet ballad of laughter and sobs escaping a hidden alley, let the whispered confessions of lovers paint achingly tender brushstrokes on your canvas. Every sigh, every honk, every murmured joke – they're your orchestra, waiting to conduct your words.

Hear the lilt of forgotten lullabies in the wind rustling through leaves, the echoes of ancient myths in the crash of ocean waves. Let the creak of a grandfather clock become the metronome of your narrative, the hum of a neon sign a pulsing bassline in your poem. The world is not a silent movie, it's a cacophony waiting to be composed, a vibrant score begging to be woven into the fabric of your story.

Don't just narrate, conduct. Let the rhythm of a rainstorm dictate the pace of your chase scene, the cadence of a child's skipping steps propel your protagonist forward. Infuse the raspy whisper of a dying man into your villain's monologue, the joyous chaos of a street festival into your hero's triumphant return. Your story is not just ink on paper, it's a symphony of shared experiences, a chorus of lives echoing through your own.

So open your ears, writer, let the world's music fill you to the brim. For in the symphony of human experience lies the truest authenticity, the deepest resonance. Compose with care, listen with your heart, and your words will dance, they will sing, they will become the soundtrack to a story that whispers, that shouts, that thunders with the vibrant truth of being alive.

Dare to be Different:

Don't be afraid to let your quirks and contradictions shine through. Inject your own humor, your own brand of cynicism, your own way of viewing the world. It's these oddities, these unexpected notes, that will make your voice sing in vibrant counterpoint to others.

Don't shy away from the chipped teacup melody of your voice. Let your sentences tilt on their axis, embrace the occasional grammatical pirouette. Infuse your prose with the tang of your own peculiar humor, the sardonic chuckle that lurks behind your observations. Weave cynicism not as a shroud, but as a shimmering thread, adding depth and texture to your narrative tapestry.

The chorus of voices is vast, yes, but fear not the cacophony. Let your own off-key notes become the spice in the literary stew, the unexpected riff that makes the heart drum a little faster. Don't iron out the wrinkles in your perspective, the quirks that make your characters dance to their own rhythm. Let your protagonist stutter with awkward honesty, your villain spin malicious puns, your sidekick trip over metaphors with endearing clumsiness.

Embrace the contradictions, storyteller. Be the one who sees beauty in a rusted bolt, humor in a spilled cup of coffee, wisdom in a child's nonsensical rhyme. Let your voice be a kaleidoscope of perspectives, a mosaic of borrowed styles and your own vibrant soul. For in the vibrant counterpoint of your unique melody lies the magic of your story, the spark that ignites connection and whispers, "This is different. This is me."

So sing your song, writer, even if it's off-key. Dance your steps, even if they're clumsy. The world needs the echo of your own peculiar music, the unexpected harmony that only you can compose. Be the voice that breaks the mold, the laughter that cracks the silence, the quirk that makes the symphony of literature a little more alive, a little more human, a little more you.

Read Your Story Aloud:

Hear your words dance on the wind. Read passages aloud, feeling the rhythm, the cadence, the way they rise and fall. Listen for flat notes, for paragraphs that drone instead of soar. Revise, polish, and let your story sing with its fullest, most authentic voice.

Remember, voice is a journey, not a destination. It will evolve, morph, and surprise you as your storytelling journey unfolds. Embrace the unexpected turns, the moments where your writing takes on a life of its own. That's when you know you've tapped into the true power of your narrative voice, an anthem that will resonate with readers long after the final page is turned.

Let your voice ring out. Paint your world with your unique colors, infuse your characters with your quirks, and sing your story to the world. After all, the echoes of a thousand hushed whispers can become the most powerful anthems, and your voice, my friend, is waiting to be heard.

Chapter 4: Characters

Crafting Captivating Characters - Where Ink Becomes Flesh and Blood

Ah, characters, the beating hearts of our stories! Those vibrant souls who dance within the pages, their choices etching paths through our worlds, their emotions painting the sky with laughter and tears. But how, dear storyteller, do these ink-stained phantoms morph into flesh and blood, captivating our readers with their every breath?

Archetypal Characters: Building Blocks of Fiction

Archetypes are the recurring patterns, symbols, and characters that appear across cultures and stories throughout history. These familiar faces, though varied in their incarnations, resonate with audiences because they tap into universal human experiences, emotions, and aspirations. Knowing and utilizing archetypes can be a powerful tool for writers, giving your characters instant depth and connecting your story to a vast web of existing cultural understanding.

Here are some of the most common archetypal characters encountered in fiction:

Hero/Heroine: The courageous champion who rises to meet a challenge, overcomes obstacles, and saves the day. Think Luke Skywalker, Katniss Everdeen, Odysseus, or Mulan.

Villain/Villainess: The antagonist who opposes the hero and threatens the established order. Consider Darth Vader, Voldemort, Cruella de Vil, or Loki.

Mentor/Wise Elder: The trusted guide who offers wisdom, training, and support to the hero. Think Yoda, Obi-Wan Kenobi, Mr. Miyagi, or Gandalf.

Trickster/Jester: The mischievous character who disrupts the status quo and plays with rules, often for their own amusement. Imagine Puck from Shakespeare's "A Midsummer Night's Dream", Loki in the MCU, or Bugs Bunny.

Lover/Partner: The romantic counterpart who offers emotional support and challenges the hero to grow. Think Romeo and Juliet, Elizabeth and Darcy, or Aragorn and Arwen.

Outlaw/Rebel: The character who challenges authority and fights for their own freedom or the greater good. Consider Robin Hood, Han Solo, Lisbeth Salander, or Katniss Everdeen.

Caregiver/Nurturer: The nurturing and compassionate character who provides emotional support and practical assistance. Think Mother Teresa, Samwise Gamgee, or Mary Poppins.

Everyman/Woman: The ordinary person thrust into extraordinary circumstances, representing the audience's perspective. Think Dorothy in Oz, Alice in Wonderland, or Bilbo Baggins.

Seeker/Explorer: The character driven by a quest for knowledge, truth, or a new world. Think Indiana Jones, Captain Ahab, or Amelia Earhart.

Shape-Shifter/Magician: The character who possesses extraordinary abilities or embodies mystery and transformation. Consider Mystique in X-Men, Merlin in Arthurian legend, or Gollum in "The Lord of the Rings."

Remember: Archetypes are not rigid molds. They are starting points, flexible frameworks that can be adapted and subverted to create unique and compelling characters. Experiment, twist the tropes, and don't be afraid to break the mold while building upon the familiar.

Beyond the List: Consider exploring sub-archetypes within these categories, such as the "Tragic Hero," the "Anti-Hero," the "Damsel in Distress," or the "Mad Scientist." Additionally, research archetypes specific to your chosen genre, as fantasy, sci-fi, and mystery often have their own distinct character types.

Sub-Archetypes: Adding Spice to the Familiar

Let's delve deeper into some sub-archetypes that add intriguing twists and variations to the classic character categories:

Hero/Heroine

Reluctant Hero: Thrust into the hero's mantle against their will, this character must overcome fear and self-doubt to rise to the challenge. Think Frodo Baggins in "The Lord of the Rings."

Tragic Hero: Doomed by fate or their own flaws, this character's heroic deeds come at a great personal cost. Imagine Oedipus Rex or Macbeth.

Anti-Hero: Morally ambiguous or even villainous, this hero employs questionable methods to achieve their goals. Consider Walter White in "Breaking Bad" or Deadpool.

Villain/Villainess

Fallen Hero: Once noble, this character has been corrupted by power, betrayal, or trauma. Think Anakin Skywalker in Star Wars or Lady Macbeth.

Sympathetic Villain: Driven by understandable motives or tragic circumstances, this antagonist evokes pity and even admiration alongside their villainy. Consider Loki in the MCU or Magneto in X-Men.

Joker/Trickster Villain: Chaotic and unpredictable, this villain delights in disruption and revels in sowing discord. Imagine The Joker in Batman or Loki in Norse mythology.

Mentor/Wise Elder

Unorthodox Mentor: An unconventional guide who challenges the hero with unorthodox methods. Think Yoda in "Star Wars" or Mr. Miyagi in "The Karate Kid."

Skeptical Mentor: Reluctant to trust the hero but eventually offering invaluable guidance. Consider Obi-Wan Kenobi in "Star Wars" or Morpheus in "The Matrix."

Fallen Mentor: A former hero or mentor who has lost their way, serving as a cautionary tale for the protagonist. Think Saruman in "The Lord of the Rings" or Dumbledore in "Harry Potter."

Remember: These are just a few examples, and there are endless possibilities for further exploration. Play with these sub-archetypes, blend them together, and don't be afraid to create your own entirely!

By understanding and utilizing archetypes, you can give your fiction a foundation of universal connection while still carving your own unique stories and characters.

Breathing Life into Words:

Actions Speak Louder:
Words are powerful, but deeds are louder. Let your characters' actions paint their true colors. A selfless act in the face of danger, a whispered apology after a bitter fight – these choices speak volumes, revealing the depths of their hearts and souls.

A character's actions can often reveal more than their words ever could. Let's explore this concept through the character of Liam, a seemingly stoic and unapproachable man with a mysterious past.

Throughout the story, Liam speaks little and often comes across as distant. However, his actions gradually reveal the depths of his character. In one pivotal scene, during a building fire, Liam unhesitatingly risks his life to save a child trapped inside. This selfless act, performed without a moment's hesitation, speaks louder than any words he could have uttered. It shows his bravery and the value he places on life, despite his outward demeanor.

Later, after a fierce argument with another character, Sarah, Liam's pride prevents him from verbally apologizing. However, the following day, Sarah finds her favorite flowers on her doorstep with a simple note, "I'm sorry," signed by Liam. This small, yet significant action, a whispered apology, reveals his humility and willingness to mend relationships, peeling back another layer of his complex character.

Through these actions, Liam's true nature is slowly unveiled to the reader. He is not just a silent, brooding figure, but a man with a heart capable of great courage and compassion. His actions paint a vivid portrait of his character, making him a compelling and multi-dimensional figure in the narrative.

Unmasking the Familiar

The Hero Re-Imagined: Ditch the shining armor and unwavering morals. Craft a hero riddled with doubts, haunted by past mistakes, wrestling with their own flaws. Show them stumbling, losing their way, but ultimately rising with unexpected grace, maybe.

The concept of a reimagined hero is explored with Lucas Hood from "Banshee" as an example, we explore a character deeply etched with complexities and contradictions. Lucas Hood, a former professional thief, assumes the identity of the sheriff in the small town of Banshee. His transformation from a criminal to a law enforcer presents a profound internal struggle.

Lucas is tormented by his past, a life of crime and imprisonment, which starkly contrasts with his present role as a sheriff. This duality within him is a constant battle - he is a man enforcing the law but simultaneously haunted by his lawless past. His actions, often on the edge of morality, depict a man trying to atone for his past sins while grappling with the temptations of reverting to his old ways.

His character development throughout the series is a journey of redemption and self-discovery. Lucas is far from the stereotypical hero in shining armor; he's flawed, vulnerable, and real. His evolution shows how a person can be both the hero and the anti-hero of their story, providing a rich, multi-dimensional character study.

Lucas Hood's narrative is a testament to the idea that heroes can emerge from the unlikeliest of backgrounds, and that redemption, though fraught with challenges, is attainable.

The Villain's Symphony: Villains are not one-dimensional monsters. Delve into their motivations, the pain that fueled their twisted path. Give them moments of vulnerability, glimpses of the humanity buried beneath the darkness. Make them complex, tragic, and strangely sympathetic.

Kai Proctor from "Banshee" exemplifies the multifaceted nature of a compelling villain. Once a member of an Amish community, Proctor's transformation into the town's ruthless crime lord stems from a deep-seated resentment towards his past and the rigid confines of his upbringing. This complex background creates a villain who is not just evil for evil's sake but is driven by a sense of betrayal and a desperate need to assert control over his life and surroundings.

Proctor's actions, though often brutal, are laced with a sense of tragedy. His estrangement from his family and his community reveals a vulnerable side, a man torn between the world he was born into and the one he has created for himself. His moments of quiet reflection, often in solitude, expose the humanity that still lingers within him.

He is not a villain who relishes in his misdeeds but rather one who sees them as a necessary part of his pursuit for power and validation. This duality makes Proctor a tragic figure, one who evokes a sense of empathy, despite his nefarious deeds. His complexity as a character lies in the interplay between his merciless actions and the glimpses of a man who once had the potential for a different, perhaps more virtuous, path.

The Sidekick's Spotlight: Sidekicks are no longer comic relief or one-dimensional cheerleaders. Give them their own struggles, ambitions, and moments of surprising strength. They're not just shadows of the hero; they're vital voices in the narrative chorus.

Job from "Banshee" epitomizes the evolution of the sidekick role in modern storytelling. Far from being just comic relief or a secondary character, Job stands out with his own complex identity and narrative arc. As a cross-dressing hair stylist and a genius computer hacker, Job's character transcends traditional sidekick roles, bringing depth and a unique perspective to the series.

Job's journey in "Banshee" is marked by his own struggles and ambitions, separate yet intertwined with those of the protagonist, Lucas Hood. Despite his flamboyant exterior, Job displays moments of profound strength and resilience, especially when facing the dangers and challenges in the criminal world of Banshee. His loyalty and skills are indispensable to Lucas, but his character is not defined merely by this relationship.

Job's narrative explores themes of identity, acceptance, and the quest for a sense of belonging, making him a vital voice in the series. His character development, interactions, and the challenges he faces contribute significantly to the series' depth, proving that sidekicks can be as compelling and multifaceted as the protagonists they accompany.

Dancing with the Unexpected

Unexpected Alliances:
Throw a wrench in the classic good vs. evil equation. Foster unlikely friendships, uneasy alliances, and shifting loyalties. Explore the gray areas where heroes make difficult choices and villains exhibit moments of unexpected compassion.

In "Banshee," the dynamic between Lucas Hood and Kai Proctor exemplifies the concept of unexpected alliances in storytelling. Hood, a former criminal posing as a sheriff, and Proctor, a powerful local crime lord, represent a complex interplay of good vs. evil.

Their relationship is marked by a series of uneasy alliances and shifting loyalties, transcending traditional hero-villain dynamics. For instance, in a critical moment of the series, despite their conflicting interests and past confrontations, Hood and Proctor find themselves reluctantly joining forces to combat a common enemy that threatens the town of Banshee. This alliance is uneasy and fraught with tension, highlighting the moral ambiguity of both characters.

Through this unlikely partnership, "Banshee" delves into the gray areas of morality, showing how even a criminal like Hood can strive for a form of justice, while a villain like Proctor can exhibit a warped sense of community loyalty. Their alliance challenges the viewer's perceptions, revealing layers of complexity in their characters - moments of compassion in Proctor and ruthless decisiveness in Hood.

This dynamic between Hood and Proctor in "Banshee" illustrates how unexpected alliances can enrich narratives, providing depth to characters and a more nuanced exploration of themes like morality, redemption, and survival.

Hidden Depths:

Let your characters surprise you! Plant seeds of hidden talents, buried fears, and unexpected quirks. Reveal them gradually, layer by layer, keeping your readers guessing and engaged. Remember, the most captivating characters are constantly evolving, defying expectations with every turn.

In the TV series "Banshee," the character Carrie Hopewell, also known as Anastasia Rabitov, exemplifies the concept of Hidden Depths. At first glance, Carrie appears to be a typical suburban mom and wife. However, as the series progresses, layers of her past and identity are revealed, dramatically altering the viewer's perception of her character.

Carrie's hidden depths unfold gradually, revealing her as a former notorious jewel thief with a complex past intertwined with the protagonist, Lucas Hood. Her expertise in combat and criminal undertakings, juxtaposed with her life as a mother and wife in a small town, create a multifaceted character that defies initial expectations.

This revelation of Carrie's past adds layers to her character, making her more intriguing and engaging. Her struggles to reconcile her past with her present life, her efforts to protect her family, and her internal conflicts add depth and complexity to her character, keeping the audience captivated and constantly reevaluating her.

Carrie's character in "Banshee" demonstrates how hidden depths and unexpected revelations can enrich a character, making them more dynamic and compelling for the audience.

The Power of Change:

Transformation is the heart of storytelling. Make your characters grow, learn, and adapt. Let them stumble through mistakes, confront their demons, and emerge stronger, wiser, forever changed by their journey.

Lucas Hood in "Banshee" is an embodiment of the transformative power of storytelling. Initially introduced as an unnamed ex-con, Hood assumes the identity of a murdered sheriff in the small town of Banshee. This premise sets the stage for his remarkable evolution.

Throughout the series, Hood grapples with the duality of his existence: a criminal masquerading as a lawman. His journey is marked by confrontations with his past mistakes, the law, and personal demons. Each encounter forces him to adapt, learn, and grow beyond his former self.

Hood's transformation is not just about changing his behavior; it's a profound internal journey. From seeking redemption for past crimes to protecting those he cares about, Hood's story is a tumultuous path of self-discovery and redemption. His struggles and choices lead him to a deeper understanding of himself and his role in the world.

By the series' end, Hood emerges as a character who has evolved dramatically from his initial portrayal. His journey illustrates the essence of storytelling, highlighting how characters can undergo significant changes, confront their deepest fears, and emerge forever altered by their experiences.

Remember, as a writer, archetypes are your starting point, not your prison. Embrace the unexpected, the flaws, the contradictions. Let your characters dance in the shadows and reach for the stars. For it's in the unique blend of light and darkness, the unpredictable twists and turns, that your creations will truly captivate and resonate with your readers.

We've delved into the depths of individual souls, sculpted flaws and dreams, and watched characters dance beyond archetypes. Remember, characters are the heart of your narrative, the beating drum that draws your readers in and keeps them enthralled until the very last page. Let them dance on the edge of the familiar, whisper secrets in the shadows, and shine with the unexpected brilliance of flawed, complex humanity.

Now, let's explore the alchemical crucible of relationships, where hearts collide, sparks fly, and the true essence of your characters ignites.

Beyond the Surface

From Acquaintance to Soulmate:

Relationships aren't static entities. Show them evolve, morphing from hesitant greetings to heated arguments, shared laughter to unspoken understanding. Trace the intricate dance of power dynamics, shifting loyalties, and the gradual peeling back of facades.

Relationships are not just portraits hanging on the wall, but vibrant tapestries woven with threads of time, experience, and emotion. In a story, capturing this dynamic dance is crucial to creating characters who feel real and their connections resonate with readers.

From Hesitant Greetings to Heated Arguments:

The Awkward Spark: Let the initial interactions be tentative, laced with nervous glances and stilted small talk. Hint at underlying curiosity or attraction, but build tension by keeping them at arm's length.

First Steps, First Clashes: As the acquaintance deepens, so do the possibilities for conflict. Introduce contrasting viewpoints, misinterpretations, and petty disagreements. Show how their personalities and past experiences clash, highlighting their differences while subtly hinting at the potential for connection.

The Crucible of Disagreement: Don't shy away from heated arguments. Let them raise their voices, hurl accusations, and reveal their vulnerabilities. These fiery clashes can strip away facades and expose raw emotions, laying the groundwork for deeper understanding and growth.

From Shared Laughter to Unspoken Understanding:

Finding Common Ground: As the dust settles, let them find shared interests, humor, and moments of genuine connection. Laughter becomes a bridge, dissolving tension and fostering intimacy.

The Comfort of Silence: Introduce moments of unspoken understanding, where words are superfluous and a simple glance speaks volumes. Show how their presence becomes a source of comfort, a haven where they can be themselves without judgment.

Shared Vulnerability: Vulnerability is the bedrock of a soulmate bond. Let them reveal their fears, insecurities, and past hurts to each other. Show how their acceptance and compassion nurture trust and deepen their connection.

The Intricate Dance of Power Dynamics:

Shifting Loyalties: Relationships are not power vacuums. Show how power dynamics shift throughout the narrative. Let them support each other, challenge each other, and even briefly compete. This dynamism keeps the relationship engaging and avoids stagnation.

The Pull of Independence: Even within a close bond, individuals crave their own space and goals. Show how they navigate their individual needs while maintaining the connection. This builds respect and avoids codependency.

Growth Through Compromise: Let them learn to compromise, finding solutions that benefit both of them. Show how their sacrifices and concessions strengthen the bond and demonstrate their commitment to each other.

Peeling Back the Facades:

The Unmasking of Secrets: As the relationship matures, let them reveal hidden secrets and past traumas. This vulnerability deepens their connection, allowing them to see each other in their entirety.

The Acceptance of Imperfections: Nobody is perfect. Show how they accept each other's flaws and quirks, imperfections becoming endearing rather than deal-breakers. This acceptance fosters genuine intimacy and strengthens the bond.

The Revelation of Souls: In a moment of profound intimacy, let them see each other's souls laid bare. This can be a shared experience of joy, grief, or simply a quiet realization of their deep connection. This moment becomes a turning point, solidifying their bond as soulmates.

By following these steps, you can craft relationships that transcend the page and resonate with readers. Remember, the journey from acquaintance to soulmate is not a linear path, but a beautiful, intricate dance of emotions, experiences, and growth. Embrace the complexities, the conflicts, and the quiet moments of understanding, and you'll create characters and connections that stay with your readers long after they turn the final page.

Misfits and Mayhem:

Not all bonds are forged in harmony. Embrace the friction, the clashes of opinion, the sparks that fly when unlikely souls collide. Explore the beauty of dysfunctional families, the bittersweet sting of forbidden romance, and the unexpected camaraderie born from shared adversity.

A Guide to Embracing the Flawed and Fiery

Not all stories sing lullabies of harmony. Some pulsate with the electric energy of dissonance, their characters bound not by gentle affection but by the explosive power of mismatched souls colliding. In these narratives, beauty arises from the ashes of dysfunction, and understanding blossoms from the thorns of conflict. So, let's embrace the mayhem, delve into the messy underbelly of human connection, and explore the unique charm of:

The Symphony of the Dysfunctional:

Fractured Families: Dive into the messy tapestry of family dynamics. Let estranged siblings bicker, parents grapple with past failures, and unspoken resentments simmer beneath the surface. Show how love flickers amidst the chaos, creating bonds more resilient for having weathered such storms.

Forbidden Flames: Ignite the tension of forbidden romance. Let societal taboos, family disapproval, or ethical dilemmas fuel the fire of attraction. Show how their love burns brighter for being challenged, their bond forged in the crucible of secrecy and sacrifice.

Tribe of Outcasts: Celebrate the beauty of misfits finding their tribe. Throw mismatched personalities, clashing ideologies, and unconventional talents into a melting pot. Watch as shared outsider status becomes the glue that binds them, their differences transforming into their greatest strength.

Friction and Fire: Embracing the Sparks:

Clashing Ideals: Don't shy away from ideological conflict. Let characters with opposing worldviews lock horns, their arguments crackling with intellectual heat. Show how these clashes force them to re-evaluate their beliefs, leading to growth and mutual respect.

Fiery Temperaments: Embrace the combustive power of hot-headedness. Let quick tempers flare, sparks fly, and passionate disagreements erupt. Amidst the verbal fireworks, show how their vulnerabilities shine through, leading to unexpected connection and deeper understanding.

Unlikely Partnerships: Juxtapose contrasting personalities for maximum friction. Pair the stoic with the impetuous, the cynic with the optimist, the loner with the social butterfly. Show how these mismatches spark hilarious clashes, unexpected growth, and ultimately, a unique and enduring bond.

Unexpected Camaraderie in the Face of Adversity:

Shared Scars: Forge bonds in the fires of adversity. Let shared tragedy, external threat, or a common enemy unite your misfits. Show how their individual strengths complement each other, their differences fading in the face of a greater cause.

Laughter in the Darkness: Don't shy away from humor in the face of hardship. Let gallows humor, shared misfortune, and quirky coping mechanisms bind them together. Show how laughter becomes a weapon against despair, strengthening their resolve and solidifying their connection.

Redemption Arcs: Give misfits the chance to rise above their flaws. Let their shared struggles reveal hidden depths, their past mistakes fueling present growth. Show how they become better versions of themselves, not despite their differences, but because of them.

Remember, harmony isn't the only melody that resonates. By embracing the discord, the friction, and the unexpected bonds born in the fires of chaos, you'll create stories that are bold, memorable, and deeply human. So, unleash your inner rebel, dive into the messy, magnificent depths of misfit mayhem, and watch your characters ignite the page with the sparks of their flawed, fiery connections.

The Weight of History:

Past relationships cast long shadows. Weave in echoes of old friendships, betrayals that linger in the air, and family secrets that whisper in the darkness. Let these ghosts influence your characters' choices, adding depth and emotional resonance to their interactions.

A Guide to Weaving in the Shadows of the Past

No character exists in a vacuum. Their choices, motivations, and even quirks are often shaped by the ghosts of experiences past, the echoes of relationships long gone, and the lingering weight of history. By weaving these threads into your narrative, you can add depth, complexity, and emotional resonance to your characters and their interactions.

Chapter 4: Characters

Echoes of Old Friendships:

The Lingering Sting of Betrayal: Let the memory of a broken friendship cast a long shadow. Show how the character still grapples with the hurt, the doubts, and the conflicting emotions of anger and longing. This can manifest in guardedness, trust issues, or a fear of intimacy.

The Unfinished Symphony: Introduce a character haunted by a friend lost to time or circumstance. Show how they carry the torch of their shared dreams, their memories a bittersweet melody playing in the background of their present life. This can lead to self-sacrifice, a sense of responsibility, or a yearning for closure.

The Second Chance at Connection: Allow a past friendship to blossom anew. Show how two people who once connected, but drifted apart, find their way back to each other. This can be a slow burn, a gradual rekindling of understanding, or a poignant reminder of the strength of their bond.

Betrayals that Linger in the Air:

The Scars of Broken Trust: Let the character bear the scars of a past betrayal, the memory a constant reminder of their vulnerability. This can manifest in cynicism, a reluctance to open up, or a constant need for control.

The Weight of Unfulfilled Promises: Show how a character struggles with the guilt of unfulfilled promises made to someone from their past. This can lead to self-punishment, a drive to redeem themselves, or a fear of facing the consequences.

The Forgiveness Tightrope: Introduce the opportunity for forgiveness, a chance to heal the wounds of the past. Show how the character grapples with the complexities of forgiveness, the desire for peace versus the lingering hurt.

Family Secrets Whispering in the Darkness:

The Skeletons in the Closet: Let the character be haunted by a hidden family secret, a truth buried beneath layers of silence and denial. Show how this secret shapes their choices, their fears, and their perception of their own identity.

The Cycle of Dysfunction: Explore how characters unknowingly repeat the mistakes of their ancestors, the weight of family history pulling them towards familiar patterns. This can lead to breaking free from the cycle, confronting the past, or a tragic continuation of the same story.

The Unexpected Legacy: Introduce a character who discovers a hidden family connection, a truth that rewrites their understanding of their past and present. Show how they navigate this newfound knowledge, forging new relationships or reconciling with long-held beliefs.

By weaving these threads of past relationships and unspoken histories into your narrative, you can create characters who feel real, flawed, and deeply human. Their choices will resonate with your readers, their struggles will evoke empathy, and their eventual growth will feel earned and satisfying. So, delve into the shadows of the past, embrace the whispers of history, and watch your characters come alive with the weight of their own unique stories.

Remember, the past is not merely a setting; it's a living, breathing force that shapes who your characters are and the choices they make. By using these techniques, you can transform your story from a simple narrative into a tapestry of experience, memory, and the enduring weight of history.

Beyond Words

Actions Speak Louder:
Dialogues are powerful, but the language of relationships often lies in unspoken gestures, lingering glances, and the subtle dance of body language. Paint these details with care, letting them reveal unspoken emotions and hidden complexities.

Shared Battles, Shared Victories: Bonds are forged in the fires of shared experiences. Throw your characters into trials, celebrations, and moments of quiet intimacy. Let them rely on each other, learn from each other, and discover their true selves in the crucible of these shared moments.

The Unspoken Language of Connection

Dialogue is the tip of the iceberg, but the true depths of relationships lie in the ocean of unspoken language. It's in the lingering touch, the averted gaze, the nervous fidget, the shared laugh that dissolves tension, where emotions whisper their secrets and complexities unfold. Mastering this unspoken language is key to crafting connections that resonate with your readers.

Painting with Gestures and Glances:

The Language of Touch: Let a gentle hand on the shoulder convey unspoken comfort, a clenched fist reveal simmering anger, or a lingering brush of fingers ignite unspoken desire. Show how physicality speaks volumes, often louder than words.

The Power of the Gaze: A fleeting glance can carry a world of unspoken emotion – longing, accusation, understanding, or unspoken love. Let your characters speak through their eyes, their gaze mirroring the turmoil within.

The Symphony of Body Language: Don't underestimate the power of posture, fidgeting, and facial expressions. A slumped posture can convey defeat, a proud stance defiance, and a nervous tick a hidden fear. Use these subtle cues to paint a vivid picture of your characters' inner landscapes.

Shared Battles, Shared Victories: The Crucible of Connection

Life is a tapestry woven with threads of joy, sorrow, triumph, and struggle. By throwing your characters into these shared experiences, you forge their bonds in the fires of shared emotions and collective growth.

Trials by Fire: Let them face challenges together, whether physical or emotional. Show how they rely on each other, their strengths complementing each other's weaknesses. This shared struggle fosters trust, respect, and an unbreakable camaraderie.

Celebrations of Triumph: Don't neglect the joys of shared victories. Let them revel in each other's successes, their laughter echoing through the air. These moments of shared joy solidify their bond and remind them of the strength they find in each other.

The Quiet Moments of Intimacy: Not all connections are forged in grand gestures. Show the power of quiet moments, shared meals, comfortable silences, and unspoken understanding. These intimate moments reveal the depth of their connection, a silent language woven from shared experiences and unspoken affection.

Remember, the language of relationships is not limited to words. It's a symphony of gestures, glances, and shared experiences that paint a vibrant picture of the ties that bind. By mastering this unspoken language, you'll create connections that feel real, nuanced, and deeply human, drawing your readers into the heart of your story and leaving them with a lasting impression of the characters who breathe life into it.

So, let your characters speak with their actions, their gazes, their very bodies. Throw them into the crucible of shared experiences, and let their bonds be forged not just in words, but in the silent language of connection that speaks volumes.

Breaking the Mold: Don't limit yourself to traditional dynamics. Explore mentor-mentee relationships, unlikely friendships across age gaps or social boundaries, and the quiet companionship of found family. Remember, the most captivating connections often defy expectations and blossom in unexpected corners.

Remember, architect of emotions: Relationships are the scaffolding upon which your characters climb. They are the mirrors reflecting their vulnerabilities, the catalysts for growth, the sources of both joy and heartbreak. Build them with care, layer them with complexity, and watch them come alive as the beating heart of your narrative.

Weave a tapestry of connections that captivates the soul. Let your characters find solace in shared laughter, forge strength in shared struggles, and discover their true selves in the intricate dance of relationships. Remember, it's in these collisions and entanglements that your story truly finds its heart and humanity.

From Whispers to Flesh and Blood

Sensory Spectacle: Infuse your characters with sensory details – the way their eyes crinkle when they smile, the scent of woodsmoke clinging to their clothes, the tremor in their voice when fear takes hold. Make them tangible, real enough to touch, taste, and feel their presence as they move through your world.

Mannerisms and Quirks: Give them ticks, fidgets, nervous laughter, and unexpected habits. These little quirks make them endearing, relatable, and uniquely themselves. Let these mannerisms evolve with their experiences, subtly reflecting their emotional journeys.

Inner Monologues Unmasking: Don't be afraid to peek into their minds. Through internal monologues and fleeting thoughts, reveal their hidden anxieties, unspoken desires, and the internal battles they fight between right and wrong. This intimate glimpse into their inner world fosters empathy and deepens connections with your readers.

Choices with Consequence: Make their actions matter. Let mistakes have lasting repercussions, victories earn hard-won respect, and sacrifices leave indelible marks. Remember, impactful choices not only drive the plot, but also sculpt your characters' souls and reveal their true depths.

The gravity of choice is paramount. It's not just about actions, but the ripples they create. Envision a protagonist whose decision to trust a dubious ally leads to a betrayal that alters the course of their journey. This mistake doesn't just affect the plot; it becomes a crucible for character development. Their trust, once freely given, becomes a guarded treasure, shaping their interactions and decisions moving forward.

Alternatively, consider a hero's hard-earned victory, not just in battle but in earning the respect of their peers. Such triumphs don't just add a notch to their belt; they transform them. Respect earned through perseverance instills a deeper sense of responsibility and purpose, refining their character.

Sacrifices, too, are a powerful tool. A character who gives up something precious for the greater good leaves an indelible mark on the narrative tapestry. Their sacrifice becomes a defining moment, revealing the depth of their commitment and the strength of their convictions.

These impactful choices are the heartbeat of a story, pulsing through every turn of the plot, shaping characters into multidimensional beings whose journeys resonate with the reader. They are more than just plot devices; they are the crucibles in which characters are forged and revealed in all their complexity.

Evolution, Not Stagnation: Growth is the essence of good storytelling.

Show your characters learning from their mistakes, confronting their demons, and evolving with each challenge. Even villains can surprise, exhibiting moments of redemption or hidden complexities that reshape our perception of them.

In crafting a compelling narrative, the evolution of characters stands as a cornerstone. It's not merely about their journey through the plot but their transformation within. Consider a protagonist initially riddled with insecurities, whose experiences lead to a newfound resilience. Each misstep becomes a lesson, shaping them into a character of fortitude and depth.

Likewise, explore the layers within your antagonist. Perhaps they begin as a figure of unyielding malice, but as the story progresses, glimpses of their past traumas and vulnerabilities surface. This not only humanizes them but also adds a layer of complexity, challenging the reader's initial perceptions.

The evolution should also reflect in their relationships. A bond forged through shared hardship can grow from fragile beginnings into a robust alliance, reflecting the characters' growth and their journey together. Alternatively, a seemingly unbreakable relationship might fray under the strain of evolving ideals and choices, demonstrating the dynamic nature of character interactions.

Remember, static characters may fulfill plot functions, but it's those who grow, adapt, and surprise who stay etched in the readers' memories. They mirror our own life experiences, where growth is continuous and multifaceted, making them not just characters in a story, but reflections of humanity itself.

Remember, weaver of worlds: Characters are more than words on a page; they are living, breathing reflections of humanity. Infuse them with your own quirks, vulnerabilities, and dreams. Make them stumble, make them rise, and paint their journeys with vivid details that bleed into reality.

Chapter 5: Setting

Worlds Come Alive - Where Brushstrokes Breathe and Shadows Whisper

Ah, welcome back, intrepid architect of imagination! We've built the foundations of narrative, breathed life into captivating characters, and now, it's time to unveil the stage upon which they dance. Buckle up, for we're embarking on a journey to craft settings that shimmer with detail, whisper with history, and become living, breathing characters in their own right.

First Strokes on the Canvas

Senses Symphony: Don't just describe, evoke! Let your reader feel the sting of desert wind on their skin, the salty spray of the ocean on their lips, the comforting crackle of a fire in a hearth. Paint your setting with vivid sensory details, making it a world they can taste, touch, and smell.

Use sensory adjectives and adverbs that make the reader feel and sense the very words that jump off the page. Here are some descriptors that are used in the passage that follows:

Adjectives:

- fiery (breath)
- rasping (sandpaper)
- sun-baked (skin)
- gritty (dance)
- emerald (embrace)
- salty (spray)
- electrifying (kisses)
- comforting (warmth)
- obsidian (chill)
- acrid (tang)
- metallic (tang)
- fetid (symphony)
- discordant (string quartet)
- reeking (sweetness)
- yeasty (perfume)
- icy (breath)
- primal (heartbeat)
- cool (caress)

Adverbs:

- fiercely (lash)
- sandpaper-like (rasping)
- sun-parched (lips)
- pirouetting (tendrils)
- deeper, deeper (dive)
- electrifyingly (taste)
- whispered (promise)
- discordantly (buzzing)
- rhythmically (thunder)
- reeking-sweetly (rotten fruit)
- contentedly (sigh)

Chapter 5: Setting

- cool-caressing (touch)
- furiously (trumpet)
- soul-feasting (banquet)
- maestro-touched (compose)

These are just some of the evocative adjectives and adverbs from the passage. Now let's use them:

Forget mere descriptions, for you wield a symphony of senses! Instead of telling, transport. Lash your readers with the desert's fiery breath, its wind a rasping sandpaper on sun-baked skin, a gritty dance across parched lips. Plunge them into the ocean's emerald embrace, let salty spray sting their eyes, taste like electrifying kisses on their tongues. Weave a crackling fire's lullaby, its comforting warmth a whispered promise against the obsidian chill, its smoky tendrils pirouetting with the scent of pine and crackling logs.

Dive deeper, deeper still, into the kaleidoscope of sensations. Let the acrid tang of sunbaked clay rise from your arid plains, the metallic tang of blood bloom on their tongues in the aftermath of a clash. Paint the swamp's fetid symphony – buzzing insects like a discordant string quartet, the squelch of mud underfoot a drumbeat of decay. Infuse the marketplace with the cacophony of haggling voices, a whirlwind of bargaining whispers and laughter's rhythmic thunder.

Be not a narrator, but a weaver of worlds. Make your readers shiver with the icy breath of a dragon, gag at the reeking sweetness of rotten fruit, sigh with contentment at the yeasty perfume of freshly baked bread. Transform rustling leaves into whispers of secrets, moonlight's touch a cool caress on their brows, thunder's growl a primal heartbeat in the earth.

Your world is not just ink on paper, it's a feast for the soul, a banquet of lived experiences. So let the storm clouds trumpet their fury, the canyons sing with the wind's flute, the cobblestones dance with rain's violins. Compose your world with a maestro's touch, and your readers will not just see, they will taste the dust on their tongues, feel the fire's warmth on their skin, become one with the symphony you've brought to life.

Show, Don't Tell: Let the setting become a storyteller, subtly revealing secrets and foreshadowing events. A creaking floorboard, a faded inscription on a crumbling wall, a lone crow silhouetted against the moon – these details speak volumes, adding depth and mystery to your world.

Look at this vivid example:

The ancient manor hunched on the cliff's edge, a brooding gargoyle against the bruised twilight sky. Sea-wracked bones of driftwood littered the windswept shore below, each bleached skull a grim portent of secrets swallowed by the ocean. Amelia shivered, pulling her cloak tighter against the whispering chill that seemed to emanate from the very stones.

A warped gargoyle leered above the arched doorway, its moss-coated eyes fixed on her like accusing marbles. Inside, the air hung heavy with the silence of forgotten centuries. Shadows stretched and pulsed in the flickering candlelight, morphing into misshapen creatures that skittered across dusty portraits and faded tapestries. Every creak of the floorboards, every groan of the rafters, seemed to whisper her name, drawing her deeper into the mansion's labyrinthine embrace.

A faded inscription, carved above a moldering hearth, caught her eye: "Tempestas revelat omnia," it whispered, the Latin chilling her blood. "The storm reveals all." Was it a premonition? A cryptic warning? The storm clouds, bruised and swollen, rolled in from the west, promising a night of unleashed fury.

Amelia wandered through the echoing halls, her footsteps echoing hollowly against the ancient stone. A gilt-framed portrait, cobwebbed and dust-laden, depicted a woman with eyes like the stormy sea, a cruel smile twisting her lips. Her gaze seemed to follow Amelia, a silent accusation hanging in the air. Was this one of her ancestors, trapped within the walls, their secrets whispering from the shadows?

The wind howled outside, rattling the leaded windows like tortured souls. A sudden crash sent a flock of startled birds erupting from the rafters, their panicked flapping the only sound besides the rising thrum of the storm. In the heart of the house, a hidden door groaned open, a gaping maw revealing a spiral staircase that plunged into the darkness below.

Chapter 5: Setting

Amelia, drawn by an invisible thread, stepped towards the abyss. Below, the darkness whispered promises and threats, an enigma begging to be unraveled. The storm reached a crescendo, the wind screaming like a banshee, the rain pummeling the roof like a thousand vengeful fists. With a deep breath, Amelia lit a torch, its flickering flame a tiny beacon against the encroaching darkness, and descended into the unknown, the secrets of the storm-soaked manor whispering their tales in the wind.

This is just a glimpse into the story that the setting itself suggests. By employing vivid descriptions, using evocative language, and planting subtle hints through details, you can turn your setting into an active participant in the narrative, drawing your readers in and leaving them eager to unravel the mysteries it holds. Remember, the world you create can be more than just a backdrop; it can be a character in its own right, whispering secrets and foreshadowing events, adding depth and intrigue to your story.

The World Shapes, the World Reflects

Mirrors of Setting: Let your characters be shaped by the world they inhabit. A grizzled detective in a rain-soaked city will carry different scars than a carefree spirit dancing in a sun-drenched meadow. Reflect the environment's influence in their mannerisms, speech patterns, and even their physical descriptions. Setting is not just a backdrop; it's a dynamic force that molds and defines characters. Imagine a weary detective, his life woven into the fabric of a city cloaked in perpetual rain. The gray skies and damp streets shape his outlook, his decisions marinated in cynicism and caution. His language is as sharp and jaded as the urban landscape he patrols, his eyes weary from watching shadows in alleyways, his coat heavy with the mist of countless nights.

Contrast this with a character born and raised in the rolling hills of a sunlit valley. Her words are as bright and free-flowing as the streams that crisscross her world. Her movements, unburdened and spontaneous, mirror the dance of sunlight through leaves. Her optimism is as boundless as the open sky, her spirit infused with the warmth of her surroundings.

These characters are products of their environments, their identities inseparably linked to the worlds they inhabit. Their mannerisms, choices, and even their physical appearances bear the imprint of their settings. The detective's trench coat, as much a part of him as his skeptical nature, the sun-kissed freckles of the valley girl speaking of her free-spirited life. In crafting characters, consider how their worlds shape them, making their stories richer and more authentic.

Worldbuilding Wonders: Whether it's a fantastical kingdom or a dystopian megacity, flesh out your setting with intricate details, unspoken rules, and a history that whispers through the cracks. Make it real, make it breathe, and your reader will become a willing citizen of your world.

Possibly like this glaring example:

The air in Lumina City hummed with a constant thrum, a symphony of hovercars zipping through obsidian canyons of skyscrapers, their neon underbellies painting the night sky in electric streaks. Below, the forgotten pulse of the earth beat through the cobblestone alleys, where scavengers bartered for scraps of discarded tech and whispers of rebellion danced on the wind.

Lumina City was built on the bones of a fallen sun, its once-glorious energy channeled into the city's veins, powering the floating towers of the elite and the flickering gaslight lamps that barely illuminated the underbelly. Above, the Guardians, bio-engineered giants with eyes like molten gold, patrolled the skies, their presence a constant reminder of the unspoken rule: never look up, never question the light.

But in the shadows, whispers of a different history crackled. In the crumbling library beneath the city's belly, Amelia traced her fingers along ancient scrolls, their brittle edges whispering tales of a time before the sun fell, when the earth was bathed in its golden glow and the Guardians were not instruments of control, but protectors.

The city elders, their faces etched with the secrets of the fall, spoke in hushed tones of the Forbidden Zone, a wasteland beyond the city's shimmering wall, where the sun's dying embers cast long, skeletal shadows and mutated creatures lurked in the radioactive dust. It was a place of exile, of whispered rebellion, and a beacon of hope for Amelia, a place where the truth might still flicker like a lone firefly in the darkness.

Chapter 5: Setting

She befriended a street urchin named Kai, his nimble fingers adept at both lockpicking and weaving stories. He spoke of hidden tunnels, forgotten passages beneath the city, whispers of a network of rebels who yearned to reclaim the light stolen from their ancestors. Amelia, her heart ablaze with newfound purpose, knew she couldn't stay in the shadows.

The night she decided to leave, the Guardians cast long, ominous shadows over the rooftops. A storm, born of rebellion and desperation, brewed in the air. Amelia, with Kai by her side, slipped into the labyrinthine tunnels, the whispers of the city's forgotten heart guiding their way. They emerged into the Forbidden Zone, the wind howling like a mournful dirge, the skeletal towers of the city looming like tombstones against the dying light.

In the heart of the wasteland, they found it - a hidden oasis, a haven where the sun's embers still pulsed faintly, nurturing a fragile ecosystem and a community of survivors. Here, Amelia learned the true history, the forbidden truths the Guardians sought to smother. Here, she learned of a prophecy, a child born under the dying sun who would one day reclaim the light.

Amelia's heart pounded in her chest. Was she the child of the prophecy? Could she, a girl from the shadows, bring light back to Lumina City? The future was uncertain, the path ahead treacherous, but with the whispers of the city's forgotten soul guiding her and the embers of hope flickering in her eyes, Amelia took a step forward, a lone figure against the desolate horizon, ready to fight for the light that was rightfully hers.

Lumina City, with its glittering facade and whispered secrets, was more than just a setting; it was a living, breathing world, its history etched in its cracks, its hopes and fears echoing in the wind. By making the city real, by giving it a past, a present, and a beating heart, the reader becomes not just a visitor, but a citizen, invested in its fate, ready to walk alongside Amelia as she dances on the edge of revolution, the dying embers of the sun casting long, hopeful shadows on their path.

Beyond the Paintbrush

Beyond Backdrops, the setting becomes a character: Don't let your setting be a static stage set. Make it an active participant in your story. Let weather conditions influence plot twists, historical events cast long shadows, and the very geography of your world dictate the direction of your characters' journeys.

Forget mere scenery, for your setting is a living, breathing character in its own right! Don't confine it to the dusty corners of stage directions. Weave it into the very fabric of your narrative, a potent brew of history, geography, and weather that simmers and boils, molding destinies and twisting plots.

Let a sudden sandstorm whip through your desert, not just as a backdrop to a chase scene, but as a game-changer, burying secrets, scattering allies, and resetting the very map of your hero's quest. Infuse your bustling medieval city with the echoes of past plagues, their lingering fear, a subtle tension pulsating beneath the surface, shaping alliances and fueling conspiracies. Make the treacherous mountain pass not just a scenic obstacle, but a character test, its unforgiving winds whispering doubts, its icy claws testing the mettle of your adventurers.

Your world's geography is not a canvas, it's a labyrinth. Let impassable swamps become cradles of forgotten lore, whispering secrets to those who dare navigate their tangled paths. Make hidden valleys havens for ancient cultures, their isolation shaping unique customs and beliefs that clash with the outside world. Carve rivers into veins of history, their currents carrying whispers of past conflicts and forgotten empires, guiding your characters towards destinies they cannot yet fathom.

Don't just describe, react! Let a volcanic eruption redraw the borders of your kingdom, throwing nations into chaos. Make a sudden blizzard the midwife of a revolution, its howling winds a rallying cry for the downtrodden. Infuse a shimmering aurora borealis with the whispers of ancient gods, its celestial dance guiding your explorers to mythical lands and forgotten truths.

Your setting is not a backdrop, it's a puppet master, a mischievous sprite pulling the strings of your narrative. So embrace its dynamism, its unpredictability, its raw power. Let it rain blood upon your battlefield, let tidal waves rewrite your coastline, let the very stones beneath your characters'

Chapter 5: Setting

feet pulse with the heartbeat of a world alive and ever-changing. For in this dynamic dance, in this vibrant interplay between story and setting, lies the true magic of storytelling – a world where every breath of wind whispers a plot twist, every grain of sand tells a story, and every step your characters take is a dance with the ever-shifting pulse of the world itself.

Paint your worlds with fire and ice, with history and storms, with mountains that whisper and rivers that roar. Let your setting be more than scenery, let it be a storm, a revolution, a god whispering in the wind. Let it be the living, breathing heart of your story.

Conflicts and Contradictions: Don't create bland utopias! Inject your world with internal conflicts, societal tensions, and hidden dangers. These cracks in the façade not only create interesting story dilemmas, but also add depth and realism to your setting.

Living, Breathing History: The past echoes in the present. Weave in clues of forgotten civilizations, whispers of ancient wars, and legends that linger in the air. Let the history of your world subtly influence your characters' choices and shape their understanding of the present.

Remember, artist of imagination: Settings are not merely backdrops; they are living, breathing extensions of your narrative universe. Infuse them with your own experiences, fears, and dreams. Make them vibrant, complex, and as dynamic as the characters who move through them.

Paint your world with vibrant brushstrokes. Let the wind sigh through ancient ruins, the sunlight dance on cobblestone streets, and the shadows whisper secrets of the past. Remember, your setting is not just a stage, it's a character in its own right, one that will linger in your reader's mind long after the final page is turned.

Deeper Shades of Setting:

We've laid the groundwork, painting our worlds with vibrant strokes and whispering histories into their stones. Now, let's delve deeper, explore the hidden chambers of setting, and discover how to make your world resonate with unique shades of meaning and mood.

Light and Shadow Play

Sun-Kissed Splendor and Gloomy Depths: Use light and shadow not just to paint a picture, but to evoke emotions. Bathe a bustling marketplace in warm light, highlighting the joyful chaos, while shrouding a forgotten crypt in chilling darkness, creating a palpable sense of dread. Let light and shadow guide your reader's journey, mirroring the emotional highs and lows of your characters.

Here is an example based on the concept above:

The marketplace was a kaleidoscope bathed in sun-kissed splendor. Spices shimmered like jewels in woven baskets, laughter ricocheted off sun-warmed tiles, and the air thrummed with a vibrant symphony of haggling voices. Light danced on oiled torsos, spun gold from threads of saffron, and painted the scene with a brush dipped in the hues of joy. But beneath this radiant tapestry, shadows lurked. In the narrow alleys between stalls, secrets were traded in hushed whispers, and the tang of fear mingled with the scent of cumin and cinnamon.

As dusk dipped its paintbrush into the sky, the joyous chaos gave way to a different dance of light and shadow. The bazaar's heart, once abuzz with life, became a labyrinth of looming silhouettes, the stalls transformed into crouching beasts, their wares glinting like malevolent eyes. The wind, once a playful jester, now whispered chilling secrets through the twisting alleys, and shadows stretched like inky fingers, reaching for Elara's trembling steps.

She pushed deeper, her heart a hummingbird trapped in a ribcage of fear. The crypt, a gaping maw in the city's belly, awaited, its entrance shrouded in an oppressive cloak of obsidian darkness. Each step was a descent into the abyss, the sun's warmth replaced by a clammy chill that seeped into her bones. The air grew heavy with the musty scent of decay and forgotten whispers, and the silence pressed against her ears like a suffocating shroud.

But then, a flicker. A faint, ethereal glow emanated from the crypt's depths, drawing Elara forward like a moth to a flame. It pulsed, a heartbeat in the darkness, beckoning her with a promise of answers, of secrets waiting to be unearthed. As she crossed the threshold, the faint glow intensified, revealing a hidden chamber, its walls adorned with luminous runes that pulsed with an otherworldly light. The shadows, once predators, retreated to the corners, cowed by this radiant defiance.

Elara's fear, like the encroaching darkness, was pushed back by this unexpected illumination. In that moment, the sun-kissed splendor of the marketplace and the chilling depths of the crypt merged, not in opposition, but in a dance of duality. Light and shadow, joy and fear, life and death – all woven into the tapestry of her journey, each thread pulling her closer to the truth that awaited.

So let your narrative be a canvas where light and shadow paint not just scenes, but emotions. Let them guide your readers through your world, mirroring the inner struggles of your characters. For in this dance of illumination and darkness, lies the power to evoke, to thrill, and ultimately, to reveal the beating heart of your story.

Weather's Whimsical Brush: Don't underestimate the power of a raging storm or a gentle snowfall. Let the weather become a character in its own right, reflecting the internal turmoil of your protagonists or hinting at impending danger. A sudden downpour could wash away secrets, while a scorching sun could simmer tensions to the boiling point.

An example using those concepts:

Rain lashed against the caravan walls, each drop a tiny hammer drumming out the rhythm of Amelia's unease. Inside, the air was thick with the mingled scent of wet canvas and desperation. Her fingers trembled on the paintbrush, the vibrant palette mocking her with its promise of joy when her heart was a storm-tossed vessel.

The desert, once a canvas of ochre and sienna, was now a swirling gray, the wind a banshee howling through the canyon's ribs. The sand, once a docile beast, whipped itself into a frenzy, burying tracks and shrouding the path ahead. Amelia's companions, their faces grim beneath their hooded cloaks, mirrored the storm's disquiet. They were hunters, yes, but this quarry – a rogue djinn rumored to hold dominion over the elements – was a storm they weren't sure they could weather.

As the downpour intensified, secrets began to leak like water through a cracked clay pot. A whispered argument, a flinch at a sudden gust, a flicker of fear in the depths of a hardened gaze – the storm became their interrogator, stripping away the layers of lies and revealing the raw pulse of their anxieties. Amelia, watching the drama unfold, saw her own reflection in their faces – the doubt gnawing at her, the fear of failure, a cold knot in her gut.

Then, a sudden lull. The wind held its breath, the rain paused in mid-air, and the silence pressed down like a leaden blanket. The caravan, a weary beast, stood stock-still, the tension thicker than the humid air. In the distance, a flash of lightning split the sky, illuminating the jagged maw of a hidden canyon entrance. The djinn's lair, revealed by the storm's momentary break.

But as the sun, emboldened by the reprieve, peeped through the clouds, casting long, ominous shadows, Amelia felt a different kind of heat rising. It wasn't just the sun's fiery gaze, but the simmering tension within the caravan. The storm, in its brief retreat, had stoked the flames of fear and ambition, turning her companions into a tinderbox waiting for a spark.

They entered the canyon, the silence broken only by the crunch of boots on wet sand and the ragged breaths of anticipation. The djinn, they knew, was a creature of the elements, and this sudden shift, from tempest to simmering sun, was more than just a change in the weather. It was a warning, a challenge, a promise of the scorching battles that awaited them in the heart of the storm's eye.

So Amelia, her brush held tight, stepped into the canyon's mouth, ready to face not just the djinn, but the storm that raged within her own soul. The weather, she knew, was no mere backdrop, but a force shaping their destinies, a reflection of the turmoil within, a brush painting their path with the capricious hand of fate. And as she walked, the sun beat down, a searing reminder that in this dance with the elements, the true battle would be fought not in the howling wind or the lashing rain, but in the heart of the storm that burned within.

Soundscapes and Silences: Weave a tapestry of sounds. Let the clatter of city life pulsate in the background, the chirping of crickets lull your reader into a tranquil forest, or the unsettling silence of a deserted mansion prickle their skin. Remember, silence can be just as evocative as sound, amplifying tension and anticipation.

"The impenetrable eeriness of silence fell over what was once the cacophony of

jungle animals, something menacing must be near."

Sensory Symphony

Beyond the Surface: Go beyond the obvious sights and sounds. Let your reader feel the rough bark of a centuries-old tree, the sticky dust of an abandoned library, the pungent aroma of spices in a bustling market. These tactile and olfactory details immerse your reader in the world, blurring the lines between fiction and reality.

Consider the following example:

Elena pressed her palm against the gnarled oak, its bark rough and cool like the scales of a slumbering dragon. Centuries whispered in the grooves, each knot a testament to storms weathered and seasons turned. Her fingers traced the ancient inscription carved into the wood – a forgotten language, its meaning as lost as the whispers of the wind through the leaves.

She inhaled the scent of the forest, a heady brew of damp earth, decaying leaves, and the sharp tang of pine needles. It clung to her hair, burrowed into her clothes, a tangible presence that wrapped her in its mossy embrace. The sun, filtered through the canopy, painted dappled patterns on the forest floor, shifting mosaics of light and shadow that danced on her skin like playful fireflies.

Stepping into the abandoned library, silence cloaked her like a moth-eaten shawl. Dust motes danced in the shafts of sunlight piercing through grimy panes, swirling in a silent waltz to the rhythm of Elena's own heartbeat. The air hung heavy with the musty scent of forgotten knowledge, a pungent blend of aged paper, leather bindings, and the faint whisper of ink. Each book, a tomb of stories untold, stood sentinel on dusty shelves, their spines whispering secrets in forgotten tongues.

She ran her fingers along a leather-bound tome, its surface cool and smooth, worn by countless hands seeking wisdom within. The scent of old paper, a dusty caress, tickled her nose, promising tales of heroes and monsters, of empires built and dreams shattered. The ink, faded with time, bled onto her fingertips, staining them with the ghosts of forgotten narratives.

In the bustling marketplace, the symphony of spices was an assault on her senses. Turmeric's earthy warmth mingled with the fiery sting of chilies, the sweet perfume of cardamom dancing with the sharp tang of ginger. Each aroma, a memory in its own right, conjuring visions of faraway lands and sun-drenched fields. The sticky dust, kicked up by sandaled feet and laden with the fragrance of cinnamon and cloves, coated her skin, a tactile reminder of the vibrant life pulsating around her.

Elena navigated the throng, her fingers brushing against the rough-hewn bowls overflowing with jewel-toned spices, their textures like whispers against her skin. The cacophony of haggling voices, the laughter of children, the rhythmic clang of metal, all wove into a tapestry of human experience, a vibrant song pulsating through the very heart of the marketplace.

In this world, Elena wasn't just a visitor; she was a participant. The sights, sounds, and smells were not mere descriptions; they were threads woven into the fabric of her experience, blurring the lines between observer and observed. She was not just reading the story; she was living it, breathing it, feeling it with every fiber of her being.

And in this sensory feast, in this immersive dance with the world around her, Elena discovered something profound – that the true magic of storytelling lay not in the words themselves, but in the experience they evoked, in the way they transported you to another place, another time, and made you feel, truly feel, as if you were there. And in that moment, with the scent of spices clinging to her skin and the whispers of the ancient oak echoing in her ears, Elena knew she had become more than just a reader; she had become a storyteller, weaving her own tale with the threads of the world around her.

Taste and Texture: Don't be afraid to evoke taste and texture. Describe the sweetness of a forbidden fruit, the grit of sand between your teeth, the comforting warmth of a freshly baked loaf of bread. These details ground your reader in the moment, making the world sensually tangible.

Memories and Metaphors: Link your setting to your characters' emotions through evocative metaphors and sensory memories. A character's childhood home might smell of freshly cut grass and baking cookies, evoking feelings of nostalgia and security. Conversely, a dark alleyway might reek of damp stone and garbage, mirroring their fear and uncertainty.

An example:

Rain lashed against the windows like a vengeful chorus, each drop a tiny drumbeat against the rhythm of Maya's mounting anxiety. The once-cozy attic, her childhood haven, now felt like a cramped attic of the mind, cobwebbed with forgotten fears and haunted by the ghosts of unlived dreams.

The dusty scent of old books, once a comforting perfume of possibility, now hung heavy, each musty page a whisper of missed adventures, unclimbed mountains, and stories left unwritten. The floorboards creaked like arthritic joints, each groan echoing the ache of regret in her own bones. The shadows, long-limbed and mischievous in her youth, now stretched into menacing claws, scraping against the walls, threatening to snatch away the flickering candlelight of hope.

She clutched a faded photograph, its edges softened by countless thumb-strokes. The image – her younger self, grinning with sun-kissed cheeks, hair a tangled halo of dandelion wishes – felt like a relic from another life, a world bathed in the golden glow of summer, where laughter danced on the wind and dreams bloomed like wildflowers.

A sudden crack of thunder, a guttural roar that rattled the rafters, sent a shiver down her spine. The attic, once a cozy nest of creativity, now felt like a storm-tossed ship, buffeted by the waves of her own uncertainty. The warmth of the photograph, a fragile ember in the icy grip of fear, threatened to flicker out.

But then, a memory, a whisper from the windblown meadows of her youth. Her grandmother, eyes twinkling with mischief, weaving tales of fire-breathing dragons and brave princesses, her voice a warm embrace in the face of childhood fears. The attic, transformed by the memory, became a stage, the creaking floorboards a rhythmic drumbeat, the shadows dancing partners rather than lurking predators.

With trembling fingers, Maya reached for a pen, its tip a needle pricking the fabric of her fear. The blank page, once a daunting white void, became a canvas, waiting to be splashed with the colors of her rediscovered courage.

The rain, no longer a dirge of doubt, became the drumroll of a new beginning, each drop a punctuation mark in the story she was about to write.

And as she wrote, the attic filled with a different kind of light, not the flickering flame of a candle, but the radiant glow of a soul rekindled. The shadows retreated, replaced by the ghosts of forgotten dreams, now dancing with the ink on the page, weaving themselves into a tapestry of hope and possibility. The attic, no longer a prison of the past, became a launchpad for the future, a testament to the power of memory and the transformative magic of a single, brave story.

For Maya knew, in that rain-soaked attic, that the true treasures weren't the dusty trinkets of the past, but the stories yet to be written, the dreams yet to be chased, the courage yet to be found, one word, one brushstroke, one memory at a time. And in that moment, the attic, once a mausoleum of regrets, became a cathedral of hope, its rafters echoing not with the creaking of age, but with the thrilling hum of a story waiting to be told.

Unleash the hidden potential of your world. Let sunbeams dance with echoes of the past, the whispering wind carry secrets in its breeze, and the very ground thrum with the pulse of its unique identity. Remember, your setting is an orchestra waiting to be conducted, a canvas begging for your vibrant strokes.

Chapter 5: Setting

Part 2: Mastering the Tools of the Trade

Chapter 6: Plot

Plotting Your Path - From brainstorming to outlining:

Now, we've laid the foundations of our narrative world, breathed life into captivating characters, and painted landscapes that shimmer with detail. Now, it's time to embark on the grand quest of plot, the map that guides our characters through triumphs and trials, twists and turns that leave readers breathless.

Plot is an intricate dance, one that needs focus and stability, yet its twists and turns need to feel uncertain, unpredictable. This can be achieved with a comprehensive outline that is a must for the story to take shape like a recipe for an incredible dessert.

Here is an example of an outline that might be created for a novel:

Part I: Foundations

Chapter 1-3: Worldbuilding

- Establish the setting: time period, location, social/political systems
- Introduce key factions and their dynamics
- Describe the environment and its significance

Chapter 4-6: Character Introductions
  Meet the protagonist(s) and their goals/motivations
  Introduce secondary characters and their relationships to the protagonist
  Showcase individual personalities and conflicts

Chapter 7-9: Inciting Incident & Rising Action
  Disrupt the protagonist's life with a major event
  Raise the stakes and force the protagonist to act
  Introduce the main conflict and antagonist(s)

Part II: Journey & Transformation

Chapter 10-12: Obstacles & Choices
  Present the protagonist with challenges and difficult decisions
  Explore internal conflicts and growth through failures and successes
  Develop relationships and alliances

Chapter 13-15: Midpoint Twist & Consequences
  Introduce a major plot twist that changes the game
  Raise the stakes and force the protagonist to adapt
  Reveal shocking truths or expose hidden alliances

Chapter 16-18: Darkest Hour & Turning Point
  Throw the protagonist into their darkest moment
  Force a choice that defines their character and path
  Set the stage for the final confrontation
  Part III: Resolution & Revelation

Chapter 19-21: Climax & Resolution
  Deliver a satisfying showdown or confrontation
  Resolve the main conflict and answer key questions
  Allow the protagonist to achieve their goals or learn valuable lessons

Chapter 22-24: Epilogue & New Beginnings
  Show the consequences of the protagonist's actions
  Offer closure and a glimpse into the future
  Leave room for reflection and open ends

Additional Tips:
  Each chapter should have a clear purpose and drive the story forward.
  Use subplots and secondary characters to enrich the narrative.
  Consider pacing and cliffhangers to keep readers engaged.
  Leave room for flexibility and adjust the outline as the story develops.
  Remember, this is just a general template. Tailor it to your specific story and its unique needs. The most important thing is to create an outline that helps you tell your story in the most compelling way possible.

The Spark's Ignition: Every journey begins with a spark, a central conflict that ignites the narrative engine. It could be a looming war, a desperate search for a missing loved one, or a character's internal struggle against their own demons. Define this conflict clearly, let it simmer beneath the surface, and watch it propel your characters forward.

Whispers of Stakes: What's at risk? Make the cost of failure tangible, raise the stakes high enough to keep your reader's heart pounding. A lost kingdom, a broken love, the very fate of humanity—these high stakes add urgency and emotional weight to your plot, ensuring your readers are as invested in the journey as your characters.

The Map Unfolds: Don't let your characters wander aimlessly in the narrative wilderness. Craft a roadmap, a loose outline of key plot points, turning points, and the ultimate climax. This roadmap gives your story direction, ensures a satisfying arc of tension, and prevents frustrating narrative detours.

Beyond the Straight Path

Embrace the Detours: Remember, the most captivating journeys are rarely straight lines. Weave in unexpected twists, red herrings, and moments of serendipity that keep your reader guessing. Throw in a chance encounter with a mysterious stranger, a sudden storm that alters the course, or a hidden betrayal that shatters trust.

Subplots Symphony: Don't let your main storyline be a lonely melody. Craft subplots like shimmering tributaries, drawing your reader deeper into the world, adding layers of complexity and surprise. Subplots can reveal hidden motivations, introduce new perspectives, and ultimately enrich the tapestry of your narrative.

Foreshadowing's Whisper: Plant seeds, leave clues, and hint at hidden dangers to come. Foreshadowing is a subtle art, a whisper in the wind that piques the reader's curiosity without giving away the game. Let breadcrumbs of information lead your reader on a tantalizing chase, eager to unravel the mysteries you've woven.

Remember, architect of narrative: Plot is not a rigid cage, but a flexible compass. Embrace the unexpected, the twists and turns, the detours that lead to hidden wonders. Craft a map that guides your characters and your readers on a journey filled with suspense, surprise, and ultimately, a satisfying sense of resolution.

Plot your path with the audacity of a daring explorer. Let unexpected storms test your characters' resolve, hidden caves reveal forgotten secrets, and the whispers of foreshadowing lead you all to a climax that resonates long after the final page is turned. Remember, your plot is the compass that guides your narrative, the backbone that gives your story structure and the thrill of an unpredictable adventure.

Weaving Tension's Tapestry: Where Every Thread Breathes Suspense

To the workshop where chapters morph into cliffhangers! We've laid the foundation of our plot, charted a roadmap with twists and turns, and now it's time to delve deeper, exploring the intricate art of weaving tension into the very fabric of your narrative. Remember, dear storyteller, that suspense is not just about plot devices, it's a symphony of elements that keep your reader's heart pounding until the very last chord fades.

Ticking Clocks and Ticking Hearts

Deadlines Dance: Inject your story with ticking clocks, impending deadlines, and prophecies whispering of doom. Let urgency crackle in the air, propelling your characters forward as time threatens to slip through their fingers. A ticking bomb, a looming election, a prophecy fulfilled within a lunar cycle – these temporal pressures keep your reader on the edge of their seat, desperate to see if your heroes can outrun the inevitable.

Peril's Poignant Palette: Don't shy away from danger. Craft moments of physical threats, moral dilemmas, and emotional turmoil. Let your characters face insurmountable odds, witness acts of betrayal, and grapple with the potential loss of loved ones. These moments of peril amplify the stakes, reminding your reader that your world is alive, unpredictable, and fraught with potential heartbreak.

Uncertain Footsteps: Keep your reader guessing! Plant seeds of doubt, sprinkle in red herrings, and leave questions lingering in the air. Is that ally a secret traitor? Was the murder an act of malice or self-defense? Are these echoes of the past mere coincidence or harbingers of a brewing storm? Uncertainty keeps your reader engaged, actively piecing together the puzzle, their mind working in tandem with your narrative.

Beyond the Surface

Internal Echoes: Remember, tension isn't always external. Delve into the inner turmoil of your characters. Let fear gnaw at their hearts, doubts whisper in their minds, and conflicting desires battle for dominance. These internal struggles create a different kind of suspense, one that draws your reader into the emotional landscape of your protagonist, their anxieties mirroring your own.

The Power of Foreshadowing: Drop subtle hints, plant whispers of impending danger, and weave in seemingly insignificant details that take on new meaning later. Foreshadowing builds anticipation, creates a sense of unease, and makes your reader feel like a detective, eagerly uncovering the secrets you've hidden in plain sight.

Pacing's Perfect Pitch: Tension is a delicate dance. Let your story breathe, allow moments of quiet reflection to punctuate the bursts of adrenaline. But remember, momentum is your friend. Don't linger too long in the lull, keep the narrative pulsing, and ensure your pacing builds towards that ultimate crescendo, the climax that leaves your reader breathless and eager for more.

Remember, master of suspense: Weaving tension is not about cheap tricks or predictable shocks. It's about crafting a story that resonates with your reader on multiple levels, playing on their anxieties, hopes, and curiosity. Let every element, from ticking clocks to internal struggles, contribute to the tapestry of suspense, ensuring your narrative grips your reader from the first page to the last.

Tap into the architect of suspense within. Let ticking clocks echo in your chapters, whispers of danger dance in the shadows, and the tapestry of your plot leave your reader breathless with anticipation. Remember, tension is the lifeblood of a thrilling narrative, the magic ingredient that transforms words into an adrenaline-fueled adventure.

Chapter 7: Dialogue

Dialogue's Dance - Where Words Become Music and Meaning Sings

Now let's venture where characters find their voices and stories pulse with the rhythms of dialogue! We've built worlds, plotted paths, and woven tension's tapestry, and now it's time to breathe life into the very heart of your narrative – the captivating dance of dialogue. Remember, dear storyteller, that words are not mere tools, they are instruments, each sentence a note in the symphony of your characters' souls.

Beyond the Transcript

Echoes of Essence: Dialogue is not just information exchange, it's a window to the soul. Let your characters' words reveal their personalities, quirks, and hidden vulnerabilities. A gruff detective's clipped sentences, a child's wide-eyed wonder, a lover's whispered endearments – these unique voices paint vivid portraits and draw your reader deeper into their motivations.

Weaving Words into Story: Crafting Dialogue that Sings

Dialogue, the lifeblood of storytelling, brings characters to life, breathes depth into your world, and propels your narrative forward. But mere words exchanged cannot hold a candle to truly woven dialogue, where every utterance resonates with the soul of your story. Here's how to transform your conversations into tapestries that capture your reader's heart:

1. Make it Sing to the Character:

Voice & Personality: Each character should have a unique voice, shaped by their background, age, and quirks. A gruff detective's clipped sentences wouldn't suit a flamboyant musician. Let their personalities shine through vocabulary, sentence structure, and even slang.

Motivation & Emotion: Dialogue reveals what lies beneath the surface. Is your character hiding vulnerability beneath sarcasm? Does anger simmer beneath their forced calmness? Let their words betray their true feelings, adding layers of complexity and intrigue.

Subtext & Nuance: Not everything needs to be spelled out. A well-placed pause, a suggestive glance, or an unspoken truth can speak volumes. Trust your reader to pick up on subtle cues and savor the unspoken conversation between the lines.

2. Let it Breathe with the Story:

Plot Progression: Dialogue shouldn't exist in a vacuum. Use it to move the story forward, reveal vital information, or trigger crucial choices. Every exchange should contribute to the narrative arc, keeping the reader invested and eager for the next word.

Worldbuilding Whispers: Don't neglect the power of casual mentions and shared references. Embed details about your world, its history, and its social dynamics into everyday conversations, painting a vivid picture without resorting to exposition.

Theme & Resonance: Let your dialogue echo the central themes of your story. A coming-of-age tale might be peppered with naive questions and hesitant pronouncements, while a dark thriller could crackle with veiled threats and cryptic warnings. Align the tone and content of your conversations with the heart of your narrative.

3. Show, Don't Tell:

Action Speaks Louder: Don't let your characters merely describe their emotions. Show them through their actions, reactions, and physicality. A clenched fist reveals suppressed anger, a nervous laugh betrays hidden fear. Let the nuances of body language complement and enrich your dialogue.

Sensory Immersion: Engage your reader's senses. Describe the sound of rain drumming on the window as they huddle inside, the taste of bitter coffee lingering after a tense conversation, the scent of dust motes dancing in a sunbeam as they exchange secrets. Sensory details add texture and reality to your dialogue, drawing the reader deeper into the scene.

Silence is Golden: Remember, not everything needs to be said. Sometimes, the most powerful moments are born from unspoken tension, pregnant pauses, and unspoken understanding. Embrace the power of silence as a storytelling tool, letting it speak volumes when words fail.

Weaving dialogue is an art, not a science. Experiment, listen to the rhythm of your characters' voices, and trust your instincts. When your characters' words resonate with the soul of your story, you'll create conversations that linger long after the page is turned, leaving your reader with the echo of a tale not just spoken, but truly woven into the fabric of your narrative.

Remember, good dialogue is more than just words on a page. It's a dance between characters, a brushstroke in your world-building, and a whisper of your story's soul. So, grab your pen, unleash your characters' voices, and let the symphony of your dialogue weave its magic on your readers.

Here is a dialogue driven example:

In the dusty attic, moonlight speared through a grimy skylight, illuminating the hunched figure of Professor Elara Silversong. Her fingers, knobbly and worn, traced the ancient script on a crumbling papyrus scroll, her lips moving silently in translation.

Across the cluttered room, perched on a precarious stack of leather-bound tomes, sat Finnigan. He was twelve, all gangly limbs and boundless curiosity, his eyes reflecting the silver moonlight like Elara's own.

"What does it say, Professor?" he whispered, his voice barely a rustle in the stillness.

Elara sighed, the sound as dry as wind through parchment. "It's a fragment, Finnigan," she rasped, her voice gravelly with age. "A story from a forgotten age, whispered on the wind of time."

Finnigan scooted closer, his knees bumping the rickety bookshelf. "What kind of story? About dragons? Or buried treasure?"

Elara chuckled, a brittle sound that dusted the air with cobwebs. "No dragons, lad, nor glittering jewels. This is a tale of whispers, of shadows dancing on the edge of perception."

"Whispers?" Finnigan frowned, his brow furrowing like a miniature mountain range. "But whispers can't tell a story, can they?"

Elara's eyes, usually the dull pewter of an overcast sky, gleamed with a sudden fire. "Ah, but they do, Finnigan. Every rustle of leaves, every creak of a floorboard, they all whisper tales, if you have the ears to hear."

She held up the scroll, the fragile papyrus trembling in her grasp. "Even the stars,' it says, shall sing their secrets to those who listen with their hearts.'"

Finnigan's eyes widened, the silver moonlight pooling in their depths. He looked around the attic, no longer a dusty haven of forgotten things, but a stage upon which whispered secrets danced. He heard the floorboards groan beneath his weight, the wind sighing through the rafters, each sound a fragment of a long-forgotten story.

"I want to hear them," he whispered, his voice barely a breath.

Chapter 7: Dialogue

Elara smiled, a fragile bloom in the gloom. "Then listen, Finnigan," she said, her voice soft as falling leaves. "Listen with your heart, and the wind will sing its secrets, the shadows will weave their tales, and even the whispers will tell their stories."

And so they sat, bathed in moonlight and whispers, the grizzled professor and the wide-eyed boy, bound by the intangible threads of a story told not in words, but in the echoes of existence itself. In that dusty attic, where time danced with shadows and secrets, the language of whispers revealed its magic, drawing them both deeper into the labyrinthine heart of a tale older than time itself.

Rhythm and Revelation: Listen to the music of your characters' speech. Consider their cadence, their vocabulary, their pauses and hesitations. A quick-witted scholar's rapid-fire banter, a weary soldier's gravelly pronouncements, a shy village girl's halting whispers – these rhythmic variations add authenticity and emotional depth to their interactions.

Not everything needs to be spelled out. Let unspoken tensions simmer beneath the surface, hints of unspoken desires flitting between the lines. A raised eyebrow, a lingering glance, a pregnant pause – these subtle cues spark the reader's imagination, inviting them to become co-creators of meaning and nuance.

Don't let your characters merely recite facts and exposition. Embed information within the flow of conversation, weave backstory into casual anecdotes, and reveal motivations through passionate arguments. Show, don't tell, and let your dialogue become a natural extension of your characters' lived experiences and emotional states.

Dialogue never exists in a vacuum. Let your characters' physical actions punctuate their words, adding layers of meaning and emotional resonance. A clenched fist during a heated debate, a hesitant touch during a tender confession, a nervous laugh masking fear – these nonverbal cues enrich the dialogue, creating a multi-sensory experience for your reader.

Sometimes, the most powerful conversations happen in the space between words. Don't shy away from the pregnant pause, the unspoken tension that hangs heavy in the air. Let silence linger, speak volumes about unspoken emotions, and allow your reader to fill the void with their own interpretations.

Remember, dialogue is the heart of your narrative, the bridge between your characters and your reader. Treat it with respect, craft it with care, and weave it into the tapestry of your story like a vibrant thread. Remember, words are not just notes, they are emotions, motivations, and revelations waiting to be sung.

Orchestrate the dance of dialogue. Let your characters' voices ring out with individuality, their rhythms echo with unspoken desires, and their silences speak volumes about the unspoken depths of their hearts. Remember, dialogue is not just information exchange, it's a symphony of souls, the very lifeblood of your narrative.

Chapter 8: Nuance of Time

Time's Tapestry - Where Past and Present Weave a Present Dance

Weaving the story with the time elements of past and present, where memories of the past whisper and the echoes of history reverberate in the present! We've built worlds, plotted paths, woven tension's tapestry, and breathed life into dialogue's dance. Now, it's time to delve into the intricate art of weaving time itself, exploring how the past and present entwine to create a vibrant, nuanced tapestry in your narrative.

Past's Poignant Palette

Don't let the past be a dusty museum relic. Weave it into the fabric of your present, through subtle hints, recurring symbols, and echoes of forgotten events. A crumbling ruin whispering of ancient battles, a family heirloom carrying the weight of generations, a recurring symbol like a broken mirror hinting at past betrayals – these threads of the past add depth, mystery, and emotional resonance to your present narrative.

A possible example:

Rain lashed against the grimy windowpane, blurring the world outside

into a watercolor smudge. Inside, the fire crackled merrily, casting dancing shadows on the stone walls of the old tavern. Amelia sat hunched over a tankard of ale, her brow furrowed as she traced the faded inscription on the wooden table: "Tempus Fugit," it whispered, "Time Flees."

Across from her, perched on a stool like a wizened raven, sat Silas, the tavern keeper. His face, etched with the map of a life well-lived, held a familiar sadness in its depths. A grandfather clock ticked in the corner, its brass pendulum swinging like a metronome to the rhythm of the storm.

"Do you ever feel it?" Amelia asked, her voice barely above a whisper. "The weight of the past, clinging like cobwebs to these old stones?"

Silas chuckled, the sound like dry leaves rustling in the wind. "Every grain of sand in this hourglass holds a story, lass," he said, gesturing to the hourglass beside the clock. "Some whispers are faint, mere echoes in the tavern rafters. But others, they cling to the very air we breathe."

He pointed to a tarnished silver locket hanging above the bar, its surface scarred and scratched. "That belonged to Elara, the Moon Weaver," he said, his voice hushed. "They say she could paint stories in the moonlight, weave dreams into reality."

Amelia's gaze drifted to the locket, a strange pull drawing her in. She had always felt an affinity for the forgotten corners of the tavern, the whispers that seemed to emanate from the worn furniture, the faded portraits lining the walls.

"But Elara vanished," Amelia said, her voice echoing the emptiness in the tavern. "Swallowed by the storm, they say. Lost in the sands of time."

Silas's eyes, the color of storm-tossed seas, held a flicker of something ancient. "Lost, perhaps," he said, his voice low. "But not forgotten. The whispers still dance on the wind, carried on the backs of moonbeams. Sometimes, on nights like this, when the rain drums a mournful rhythm, I hear them."

He leaned closer, his voice barely a breath. "They speak of a hidden door, veiled by shadows, leading to a forgotten realm where time stands still. A place where Elara waits, her stories woven into the very fabric of the moonlit world."

Chapter 8: Nuance of Time

Amelia felt a shiver crawl down her spine, a mix of fear and excitement. Was Silas just weaving another of his tavern tales, or was there truth whispering beneath the surface?

"And you?" she asked, her voice barely a whisper. "Have you seen this hidden door? This realm where time stands still?"

Silas closed his eyes, his weathered face softened by the firelight. "Perhaps, lass," he said, his voice a mere sigh. "Perhaps. But some doors are meant to be left unopened. The past is a powerful tide, and it can pull you under if you're not careful."

He opened his eyes, their depths meeting hers. "But for those who dare to listen," he said, a hint of a smile playing on his lips, "the whispers of the past can lead to the most extraordinary adventures."

And as the storm raged outside, and the clock ticked its relentless rhythm, Amelia knew that the whispers in the wind were no longer just a tavern legend. They were a call, a siren song beckoning her to unravel the mysteries of the past, to face the shadows that clung to the present, and perhaps, just perhaps, find her own way through the hidden door, into the realm where time stood still.

The whispers of the past had awoken within her, and Amelia knew she could no longer ignore their call. The adventure, it seemed, had just begun.

The past shapes who we are. Let your characters bear the scars of their histories, both physical and emotional. A war veteran haunted by PTSD, a child prodigy burdened by expectations, a ruler wrestling with the shadow of a tyrannical predecessor – these echoes of the past fuel conflicts, motivate choices, and make your characters more than just players in the present moment.

Not all the past is static. Let remnants of forgotten lore resurface, hidden truths be unearthed, and lost legacies rediscovered. A dusty journal revealing a family secret, a forgotten prophecy pointing towards the future, a long-lost treasure sparking renewed conflict – these moments of rediscovery not only enrich the present but also offer thrilling plot twists and opportunities for character growth.

Beyond the Hourglass

Present's Poignant Pulse: Don't get lost in the shadows of the past. Keep your present narrative vibrant, infused with the immediacy of emotions, the urgency of challenges, and the unexpected turns of fate. Let your characters grapple with present conflicts, forge new relationships, and make choices that will shape their destinies and the world around them.

Past's Present Influence: Remember, the past isn't just a backdrop. Let it actively influence the present. Unresolved conflicts resurfacing, old grudges igniting new flames, traditions clashing with progress – these ripple effects of the past add complexity, create tension, and drive the plot forward with the weight of history behind it.

Breaking the Cycle: Not all characters are bound by their past. Allow them to challenge old narratives, rewrite family legacies, and choose their own paths. A prodigal son breaking free from expectations, a victim of prejudice overcoming past injustices, a community healing from historical wounds – these acts of defiance against the past offer hope, redemption, and the possibility of a brighter future.

Remember, weaver of timelines: Time is not a linear line, but a tapestry woven with threads of past, present, and future. Embrace the echoes of history, let them inform your characters, and weave them into the fabric of your narrative with intention and nuance. Remember, the past is not just a prologue, it's a living force that shapes the present and whispers promises of the future.

Become the master of time's tapestry. Let ancient ruins whisper forgotten secrets, prophecies from the past cast shadows on the future, and your characters break free from the shackles of history to forge their own destinies. Remember, time is not just a setting, it's a powerful tool in your narrative arsenal, one that can add depth, complexity, and a sense of poignant inevitability to your story.

Chapter 8: Nuance of Time

Try something like this:

The wind howled through the crumbling archway, a mournful chorus echoing off the cracked stones of the forgotten city. Amara, her cloak billowing in the gale, stood poised at the precipice of the past, her gaze fixed on the faded inscription etched above the arch: "Tempus Rex," it proclaimed, "Time, the King."

Behind her, Kai, his eyes wide with a mix of trepidation and awe, adjusted the pack strapped to his back. "Are you sure about this, Amara?" he whispered, his voice barely audible over the wind's song. "The Oracle's prophecy spoke of a 'path through time,' but this... this feels like a leap into the abyss."

Amara turned, her face etched with the same conflicting emotions. "I know," she confessed, her voice raspy with the weight of their journey. "But the whispers in the wind, Kai, they grow louder with each passing day. They speak of a forgotten truth, a hidden key to breaking the curse that binds our future."

The curse. It had shackled their kingdom for generations, a perpetual twilight cast by a long-forgotten sorcerer. The whispers, born from crumbling temples and ancient scrolls, hinted at a lost ritual, a prophecy whispered through the ages, and a hidden valley where time itself stood still.

Kai's hand tightened on the hilt of his sword. "But the valley, it's just legend, Amara. A fairy tale told by firelight."

Amara smiled, a fleeting flicker of defiance in her eyes. "Perhaps," she conceded. "But legends have a way of bleeding into reality, especially when they're written in the blood of our ancestors."

With a deep breath, she stepped through the archway, the wind seeming to sigh in welcome. The world shifted, the stones blurring into a kaleidoscope of colors before solidifying into a verdant valley bathed in an ethereal glow. Time, here, seemed to stand still, the air heavy with an ancient silence.

They walked through fields of jade-green grass, the air thick with the scent of forgotten flowers. In the distance, a crystalline waterfall cascaded down a cliff face, its water shimmering with an otherworldly luminescence. It was a place of breathtaking beauty, yet an unsettling stillness hung in the air, a constant reminder of their precarious journey.

Suddenly, a voice, soft as the rustle of leaves, echoed through the valley. "Welcome, travelers from the sands of time."

Amara and Kai spun around, their hearts pounding in their chests. A woman stood before them, her silver hair flowing like moonlight, her eyes pools of ancient wisdom. She was the Oracle, or so the whispers had claimed.

"You seek the key," she said, her voice a mere whisper. "The key to break the chains of your future, woven in the tapestry of the past."

She gestured to a stone monolith rising from the heart of the valley, its surface etched with intricate symbols that pulsed with a faint inner light. As Amara approached, the symbols shimmered, rearranging themselves into a scene from their own history – a forgotten battle, a whispered betrayal, a king's broken vow.

The Oracle's voice, tinged with sorrow, spoke of a time when their ancestors, blinded by ambition, had sought to control the flow of time itself. The ritual, intended to grant them immortality, had instead unleashed a curse, trapping their kingdom in an endless twilight.

"Only by acknowledging the past, by facing the shadows of your history, can you break the chains of the present," the Oracle intoned.

Amara's eyes met Kai's, a silent understanding passing between them. They had come seeking a weapon, a magic spell, but what they found was a truth, a burden of responsibility. To break the curse, they had to confront the sins of their ancestors, to rewrite the tapestry of their history with threads of forgiveness and acceptance.

As the sun, a pale orb in the sky, dipped below the horizon, casting long, spectral shadows across the valley, Amara and Kai knelt before the monolith. With trembling hands, they traced the symbols, their fingers whispering apologies and promises, a silent oath to learn from the past and forge a brighter future.

The monolith pulsed, its light intensifying until it bathed the valley in a blinding luminescence. Then, with a deafening crack, it shattered, sending shards of time cascading around them. And when the light faded, Amara and Kai found themselves back in the ruins, the wind still howling, but the weight of the past, somehow, lighter.

Chapter 8: Nuance of Time

They had not found a magic spell, but they had found something far more powerful – the courage to face their history, the strength to break free from its shackles, and the hope, born from the ashes of the past, to weave a new tapestry for their future.

Chapter 9: Description

Where Paintbrushes Dance and Senses Sing

Show, Don't Tell - Utilizing vivid description and action to bring your story to life.

Welcome back, fellow artist of imagination, to the pages where worlds bloom in vibrant detail and stories ignite the reader's senses. We've built characters that breathe, woven worlds that shimmer, and crafted dialogue that dances on the page. Now, we delve into the art of "show, don't tell," the magic trick of conjuring worlds and experiences for your reader, not through dry exposition, but through the intoxicating magic of vivid description and dynamic action.

Beyond the Blackboard

Sensory Symphony: Don't just tell your reader it's raining; let them feel the icy sting on their cheeks, hear the drumming on the rooftop, smell the petrichor rising from the parched earth. Engage all five senses, paint pictures with your words, and transport your reader into the heart of your scene.

Action's Pulse: Don't narrate a fight; make them witness it. Describe the blur of fists, the crunch of bone, the ragged breaths of exertion. Let the action unfold in real-time, thrusting your reader into the adrenaline-fueled chaos, their heart pounding in sync with your protagonist's.

Emotional Echos: Don't tell your reader your character is sad; show them the tremor in their voice, the slump of their shoulders, the glistening tear tracing a path down their cheek. Evoke emotions indirectly, through subtle details and evocative imagery, and let your reader empathize, connect, and feel alongside your characters.

Beyond the Brushstrokes

Metaphors that Mingle: Don't settle for cliches. Paint your world with fresh similes and metaphors. Let the setting sun bleed like a wound on the horizon, the heroine's anger flare like a supernova, the hero's loyalty burns like a steady hearth fire. Find unexpected comparisons, make the familiar strange, and spark your reader's imagination with vibrant linguistic landscapes.

Show, Even in Dialogue: Let your characters reveal themselves through their actions and reactions. Let the warrior flinch at a sudden noise, the scholar bites their lip in concentration, the lover touches their hair nervously. These seemingly insignificant gestures speak volumes about their personalities and emotional states, adding depth and nuance to your dialogue.

Internal Whispers, External Echoes: Don't forget the power of internal monologue. Let your reader glimpse into your characters' thoughts and anxieties, their hopes and fears. But remember, even these internal musings should show, not tell. Use sensory details, metaphorical echoes, and fragmented thoughts to create a tapestry of the mind that reflects the external world they inhabit.

Advanced Techniques

Focus Shifts: Don't get bogged down in omniscient narration. Shift your focus like a camera, zooming in on a character's trembling hand, then panning out to capture the vastness of the battlefield. These dynamic shifts in perspective keep your reader engaged, offering both intimate glances and breathtaking panoramas.

Figurative Language Fireworks: Experiment with literary devices. Weave in personification, give inanimate objects voices, and let the wind whisper secrets. Don't shy away from hyperbole, allegory, or even stream-of-consciousness to intensify emotions and paint your world with a unique brushstroke.

Show, Don't Summarize: Resist the urge to summarize events. Let your reader experience them firsthand, through vivid descriptions and dynamic action. Show them the hero infiltrating the castle, not just that they "got in." Show them the villain's chilling monologue, not just that they "made a threat." Immerse your reader in the moment, let them see, hear, and feel the story unfold without the crutch of exposition.

Remember, sculptor of scenes: "Show, don't tell" is not just a rule, it's a mantra. It's the alchemy of transforming words into experiences, of painting worlds that shimmer with detail, and of igniting the reader's senses with every scene. Embrace the power of description, let action pulse through your narrative, and remember, your words are not just ink on paper, they are a portal to a living, breathing world waiting to be explored.

Chapter 10: Points of View

Exploring different narrative perspectives

Point of View Playground: First-person, Third-person, and Second-person POV

Experiment with perspective! Let your readers inhabit your characters' minds, seeing the world through their eyes, feeling their anxieties and triumphs as their own. This intimacy, this shared journey, is what binds us to them, transforming them from ink-stained figures into companions on the adventure.

Consider a character, Alex, a young explorer in a fantastical world, whose story we will tell through varying points of view (POV).

First, we utilize the first-person POV. Alex's voice narrates his journey, immersing us in his innermost thoughts and feelings. *"I stepped into the ancient forest, my heart racing with excitement and a hint of fear. The trees seemed to whisper secrets of a bygone era, and I felt a deep connection with the untold stories of this mystical place."* This perspective allows readers to see through Alex's eyes, feel his pulse quicken, and experience his awe and trepidation.

First Person POV: Unveiling the Depths of Your Story

The first-person perspective, where your readers inhabit the mind and experience the world through the eyes of a single character, holds immense power in a novel. It's a unique window into the protagonist's inner world, their thoughts, emotions, and biases, drawing the reader into a deeply personal connection with the narrative. Here's how utilizing this perspective can benefit your novel:

1. Intimacy and Empathy:

Direct Connection: First-person allows you to directly express the protagonist's thoughts and feelings, fostering an immediate bond with the reader. Their joys, fears, struggles, and triumphs become the reader's own.

Emotional Resonance: By inhabiting the protagonist's mind, readers experience their emotional world with raw intensity. You can evoke empathy, suspense, and excitement by sharing their internal monologue and reactions to events.

Unreliable Narration: This perspective can also play with reader expectations. An unreliable narrator, with hidden motives or skewed perceptions, can create a sense of mystery and tension, keeping the reader guessing about the truth and questioning the protagonist's motivations.

2. Immersing in the World:

Sensory Richness: First-person lets you describe the world through the protagonist's senses, enhancing the reader's immersion. The sights, sounds, smells, and textures they experience become vivid and personal, drawing them deeper into the setting.

Subtle Worldbuilding: This perspective allows you to reveal details about the world gradually, through the protagonist's observations and interactions. Their reactions and questions can subtly introduce social norms, history, and cultural nuances without resorting to exposition.

Pacing and Tension: You can control the pace of the story and build tension by carefully filtering information through the protagonist's awareness. Holding back crucial details or delaying their understanding can create suspense and keep the reader engaged.

3. Character Complexity and Growth:

Internal Conflict: First-person lets you showcase the protagonist's internal struggles, doubts, and motivations. Their thoughts and anxieties become visible, making them a nuanced and relatable character.

Transformation and Growth: The reader witnesses the protagonist's journey of self-discovery and growth firsthand. Their changing perspectives and evolving understanding of themselves and the world around them provide a satisfying arc for the narrative.

Multiple Voices: Consider employing multiple first-person narrators for distinct perspectives and voices, enriching your story with diverse viewpoints and creating a tapestry of interwoven narratives.

4. Challenges and Considerations:

Maintaining Voice: Ensure your protagonist's voice is consistent and distinct, reflecting their age, personality, and background. Their thoughts and expressions should feel natural and true to their character.

Pacing and Information Control: Avoid information overload. Filter events and details through the protagonist's awareness, keeping the reader engaged without bombarding them with all-knowing narration.

Avoiding Self-Indulgence: While exploring inner thoughts, ensure they serve the plot and character development. Excessive introspection or rambling can lose the reader's interest.

Remember, the first-person perspective is a powerful tool for creating intimacy, immersion, and complexity in your novel. By using it with intention and focus, you can draw your readers into a captivating experience where they live and breathe alongside your protagonist through every twist and turn of your story.

Switching to the third-person limited POV, we step back slightly, observing Alex's actions and reactions more objectively. "**Alex paused, surveying the forest. The enormity of his quest weighed on him, yet his determination shone through his furrowed brow.**" This shift offers a broader view of Alex's journey, providing insight into his character while maintaining a sense of closeness.

Exploring the Power of Third-Person Perspective

While first-person offers an intimate peek into a character's mind, third-person perspective acts as an omniscient observer, weaving a broader tapestry of your story. This versatile approach allows you to explore the world and its inhabitants from multiple angles, offering unique advantages for shaping your narrative:

1. Expansive Storytelling:

Multiple Characters: Third-person grants you the freedom to switch between characters, weaving their individual stories into a rich tapestry. You can explore diverse perspectives, motivations, and conflicts, creating a more comprehensive and dynamic world.

Worldbuilding Scope: This perspective lets you zoom in and out, showcasing both intimate moments and sweeping landscapes. You can paint a vivid picture of your setting, its history, social structures, and even the thoughts and emotions of different groups or eras.

Unveiling Mysteries: You can control the flow of information, building suspense and intrigue by revealing details at your own pace. Hints dropped for one character might remain hidden from another, creating a sense of mystery and speculation for the reader.

2. Narrative Flexibility:

Voice and Tone: You can experiment with different voices and tones for different characters, adding depth and personality to each individual. This flexibility allows you to create distinct personalities and voices that resonate with your reader.

Objectivity and Subjectivity: Third-person allows you to blend objective narration with subjective insights. You can describe events neutrally while revealing characters' hidden thoughts and emotions through their actions and reactions, offering a nuanced understanding of their motivations.

Moral Exploration: With the freedom to explore multiple perspectives, you can raise complex moral questions and present various viewpoints without needing your characters to be outright heroes or villains. This creates a more realistic and thought-provoking reading experience.

3. Creative Storytelling Devices:

Limited & Omniscient Narrator: Choose between limited third-person, where you remain close to one character's perspective, or omniscient third-

Chapter 10: Points of View

person, where you hover above the story, offering insight into all characters' thoughts and motivations. Each technique offers its own strengths and limitations, allowing you to tailor the narrative to your story's needs.

Internal Monologues & Stream of Consciousness: Even in third-person, you can delve into a character's inner world through internal monologues or stream-of-consciousness techniques. This adds depth and complexity to their persona, offering glimpses into their emotions and thought processes.

Unreliable Narrators: You can choose to employ an unreliable narrator, someone with their own biases or agendas, making the reader question the truthfulness of the information presented. This creates a sense of intrigue and keeps the reader guessing about the true nature of your characters and events.

4. Challenges and Considerations:

Maintaining Objectivity: Avoid injecting your own biases or opinions into the narration. Aim to present events and characters neutrally, allowing the reader to form their own interpretations.

Pacing and Information Control: Manage the flow of information carefully. Don't overwhelm the reader with omniscient knowledge, but also avoid leaving them feeling lost or confused. Ensure the information revealed serves the plot and character development.

Character Development: While you can show characters evolving through their actions and decisions, explicitly showcasing their internal growth can be more challenging than in first-person. Carefully balance external actions with subtle shifts in their thoughts and behaviors to convey their development convincingly.

Remember, third-person perspective is a powerful tool for weaving intricate narratives, crafting diverse characters, and exploring the world from multiple angles. Utilize its strengths, approach its challenges with awareness, and let it guide you in crafting a compelling and multi-faceted story that truly captivates your readers.

Finally, we experiment with the second-person POV, a rare but powerful tool. *"You step cautiously into the unknown, your senses alert. You feel the ancient magic of the forest, its whispers tickling the back of your mind."* This perspective directly engages the reader, making them an active participant in Alex's adventure.

Second Person POV: A Dance Between Reader and Narrative

The second-person perspective – where you directly address the reader as "you" and invite them into the protagonist's shoes – presents a unique and often daring choice for novelists. This unconventional approach can forge an immediate connection with the reader, but navigating it successfully requires careful consideration. Here's how employing this perspective can impact your novel:

1. Intimacy and Immersion:

Direct Participation: By addressing the reader as "you," you blur the line between observer and participant. The reader becomes the protagonist, experiencing the story from within, their choices and actions shaping the narrative.

Emotional Bond: This perspective fosters a deep emotional connection. The reader's heart races with the protagonist, their successes are personal victories, and their failures carry sting. It's a shared journey, heightening engagement and empathy.

Uncertain Identity: Unlike first-person, second-person allows for flexibility in the protagonist's identity. The reader can fill in the blanks, projecting their own experiences and personality onto the "you," making the story feel personalized and relatable.

2. Narrative Challenges and Techniques:

Maintaining Voice: While not explicitly voiced, the protagonist still has a distinct personality and internal world. Ensure the narrative reflects their thoughts, emotions, and biases through descriptions, actions, and reactions.

Motivation and Choice: Clearly establish the protagonist's motivations and desires. The reader needs to understand what drives them forward and why they make certain choices, even if they are not explicitly instructed.

Pacing and Information Control: Manage the flow of information carefully. Oversharing can break the illusion of participation, while withholding crucial details can frustrate the reader. Strike a balance to keep them engaged and involved.

3. Unique Storytelling Opportunities:

Experiment with Genre: Second-person shines in genres like thrillers, mysteries, and choose-your-own-adventure narratives, where the reader's active participation and uncertainty heighten the experience.

Internal Conflict Exploration: Dive deep into the protagonist's psyche. Use their internal monologue and emotional responses to explore anxieties, doubts, and moral dilemmas, creating a complex and layered character.

Unreliable Narration: Second-person can present a unique take on unreliable narrators. The reader, initially trusting their own perceptions, can be subtly manipulated or misled, creating a sense of paranoia and questioning.

4. Considerations and Cautions:

Maintaining Reader Agency: Avoid giving the reader too much control. The story still needs structure and direction, ensuring a fulfilling narrative arc.

Rhythm and Tone: Second-person narration can feel unnatural if not handled skillfully. Experiment with sentence structure, rhythm, and voice to find a tone that feels engaging and flows naturally.

Not for Every Story: Not all stories benefit from this perspective. Complex plots with multiple characters or heavy world-building can feel disjointed. Choose your moments wisely and ensure the second-person adds value to the story.

Using the second-person perspective effectively requires intentionality and creativity. When wielded skillfully, it can create a deeply immersive and personalized experience for your readers, blurring the lines between storyteller and story consumer. Embrace the challenge, find your unique voice, and let your readers dance with your narrative in a way they never anticipated.

Through these shifts in POV, Alex transforms from a mere character to a companion, his journey becoming a shared experience. Readers are no longer just observers; they're adventurers, co-exploring the narrative landscape, feeling every triumph and setback as if it were their own.

Characters aren't mere puppets spouting dialogue. They are living, breathing beings with flaws and fire in their hearts. Treat them with care, listen to their whispers, and watch them evolve. For when you breathe life into their souls, your readers will follow, hopefully, their hearts will pound in sync with your creations.

Craft a cast of characters so real, so relatable, that they leap off the page and dance into your readers' lives. Remember, they are the mirrors reflecting your world, the instruments playing your narrative melody. With each stroke of your pen, breathe life into their souls, and watch them captivate the world with their unique song.

We've explored the depths of your characters' souls, unearthed their hidden desires, and painted their imperfections with vibrant brushstrokes. Now, the informed writer can take them from shadows to spotlight, pushing beyond cookie-cutter archetypes and into the dazzling realm of nuance and surprise.

Final words

Unleashing Your Story - It's All Yours Now

As you close the final page of this guide, a bittersweet feeling washes over you. You've journeyed through the intricacies of craft, the spark of imagination, and the power of words woven into worlds. But now, a daunting precipice looms – the blank page, awaiting your unique story.

Fear not, fledgling scribe, for the tools you've acquired are not mere ink on paper. They are embers flickering within you, ready to ignite the furnace of your creativity. Remember, the most captivating stories are born not from textbook rules, but from the echo of your own experiences, dreams, and yes, even your fears.

Embrace the messiness of your first drafts, the stumbles and false starts. Each is a step on the path to finding your voice, your rhythm, your way of breathing life into characters and weaving landscapes that shimmer with possibility.

Chapter 10: Points of View

And when the world doubts, or the blank page taunts, remember the whisper of the muse within. Let it guide you through sunlit meadows and shadowed valleys, through triumphant battles and whispered secrets. Let it sing through your fingertips, etching your tale onto the canvas of the world.

This guide was merely a map, a compass to point you north. Now, take a deep breath, fling open the window of your imagination, and soar. The blank page is not a void, but a canvas, an invitation to paint your own masterpiece.

Let the world hear your story, for it is waiting, breathless and expectant, to be swept away by the magic only you can create. Go forth, writer, and weave your tale. The world needs your voice, your vision, your unique spark of storytelling.

Remember, the journey ahead is yours alone, paved with the cobblestones of your own imagination. So, write with fire in your heart, ink in your veins, and a melody of words dancing on your tongue.

This is not the end,
   but the beginning.
   Write on, emboldened one, write on.

About the Author

❦

You can connect with me on:
🌐 https://www.storyweaverbooks.com
🐦 https://twitter.com/Willem2B
📘 https://www.facebook.com/bill.hatfield.397